MY CENTURY

Virgil C. Aldrich

My Century

Copyright © 1987 by Virgil C. Aldrich

All Rights Reserved

No part of this book may be reproduced or transmitted in any form or by any means, graphic, electronic, or mechanical, including photocopying, recording, taping, or by any information storage or retrieval system, without permission in writing from the publisher.

ISBN-10: 0-557-78443-3
ISBN-13: 978-0-557-78443-1

Published by EditAndPublishYourBook.com in association with Lulu.com
Proprietor and Book Designer: Michael Wells Glueck
Email: MichaelTheAuthor@Yahoo.com

My Century

Foreword

Several decades ago, I had an opportunity to ask Virgil Aldrich what he was working on. With a shy smile I had grown to love as an undergraduate at Kenyon College, he remarked that he was writing something called *My Century*. He seemed to have doubts that anyone would wish to see it, let alone publish it. *My Century*, he said, was "too philosophical for words." Now it has been my good fortune to help bring this work to the light of day.

My Century is a remarkable book. Some of it *is* too philosophical for words. For instance, Virgil writes:

> My own person or my own life has always been a vacuous sort of nonentity, in itself. There seems to be nothing about myself in particular for me to remember when I look back. It is as if what I have been is an empty place which has been occasionally filled with the lives of other people. Not my own life. Even they have found nothing positive in me. But, in the hollow that I am, they have been activated and nourished, while I remained as nothing, a catalyst. How well I understand the existentialist talk about Nothing.... (Section 1)

These lines, from one of the kindest, wisest, and most just of men, take my breath away. Far be it from me to disagree with a revered teacher who may have been reading too much T.S. Eliot. But if Virgil was nothing in himself, then it was the kind of nothing that Socrates was: Socrates the gadfly, the mid-wife, the man whose exemplary goodness made even his hardened jailer weep.

This book is a treasure—for its humanity, for its depiction of the philosophical life, and for its active engagement with some of the most intractable problems philosophy has to offer. When Virgil affixed his copyright on *My Century*, he was almost eighty-five years of age. Still he wrote and thought as vigorously as someone half his age. Some might say that the book sounds as if it belongs to the middle of the twentieth century. Perhaps. But have we really made so much progress in solving the questions that have challenged people from the time of the Greeks? Virgil was part of that grand tradition of thinkers who lived the philosophical life because that was the only kind of life that mattered. We can still learn and take heart from that.

For many years, *My Century* was resting quietly in the Archives of the University of Utah with the rest of Virgil's papers. I did not know this until I found myself in contact with Stan Larson of the Manuscript Division of the J. Willard Marriott

Library. Not really believing that the fates would be so kind, I inquired about *My Century*. Yes, Dr. Larson said, the Aldrich Archives included it, and he agreed to send me a copy right away. Next, Dr. Bruce Haywood, another esteemed professor from my days at Kenyon, put me in touch with Michael Wells Glueck (Kenyon, 1959), who graciously gave of his time and technical expertise. Without him, *My Century* would never have appeared in an electronic format. I owe a deep debt of gratitude not only to these people, but also to Robert C. Howell (Kenyon, 1961) for sage advice, and to Robert Virdis and Sara Heller Mendelson for much aid along the way. All of them understood instinctively that honoring one's teachers takes high priority in any hierarchy of values.

A few words are in order about the transcription of *My Century*. The Archive's original is a typescript. To the extent possible, I have reproduced here a faithful copy of that original. A few typographical errors have been corrected. Here and there a comma has been added or deleted. No substantive liberties, however, have been taken. This is best exemplified by the last line of the book which at first I was tempted to delete as anticlimactic. It seems to be a note to someone who was aiding in the preparation of the final section of the book. To this unknown person, Virgil wrote: "Please get that etymological sense of 'mortify.'" To me that line has the same haunting quality as Socrates' final request to Crito at the end of the *Phaedo*.

Throughout the process of preparing *My Century*, I have thought of myself not as an editor, but as a modern amanuensis. In some respects, Virgil's work is incomplete. There are footnotes only for Section 30. Even those vary in style and informativeness. I have resisted the temptation to produce a foolish consistency where one did not exist before. Philosophy, we know, is an on-going process, incomplete by its very nature. We, Virgil's epigones, should not regard this as a deficiency, but as a spur to further thought.

Alan Mendelson (Kenyon, 1961)
Hamilton, Ontario
November, 2010

1.

I often think a bit sadly of what has happened in the world since the beginning of my life in 1903. The picture of the great developments presents itself to me as a philosophical impression that subtly illuminates them, tantalizing me with the suggestion of a philosophy of life and death, a whole philosophy. I have attempted to give it a systematic, conceptual formulation as a whole, and always failed. Parts of it I have succeeded in spelling out in published essays that satisfied the demands of philosophical precision in this age of analysis. These standards have not annoyed me as they have several colleagues of mine. Sanity and sanitation are allied even in philosophy. The cleanliness that is next to godliness in general has its special analogue in the analytical sanitation ("making sane") that is next to philosophical wisdom. Especially in an oral argument I like philosophers to come clean with what they have to say. This is a fine antidote not only for the dangerous ideological currents of thought which at present threaten all true philosophy—the rampaging ideologists hate philosophical analysis most of all—but it is good even for philosophy just as vision or metaphysical insight into the nature of things, not as ideology sparking massive collective action.

Still there is something about philosophy as vision which is better served by the method and language of suggestion than by that of explicit analysis. Philosophers given to metaphysical world-viewing, like Whitehead, Heidegger, Bergson, Hegel, Plato and others have noticed this. But the remarkable thing is that even the most influential language "analyst" of my beloved and staggering twentieth century, of which I am wholly a creature since I shall die before it ends, has noticed precisely the same thing and deliberately espoused suggestion as the method of his philosophy. Wittgenstein anxiously urged philosophers not to begin with thinking, analytical or otherwise, but with looking, seeing, vision, to avoid the perplexity of wrong and unnecessary preconceptions. Thus, for him too, vision in some sense is the ballast that preserves philosophical sanity, and analysis by itself, being a special thing, will not do in that capacity. So he also spoke and wrote suggestively about his subject-matter. He was possessed by a vision of living language, the language we live by, which is as wonderful and kaleidoscopic a phenomenon as anything. It is our form of life and death. The wisest philosophers who are captured and activated by this vision are aware of how inept it is to call the ensuing philosophical activity "language analysis," since such philosophizing is directed by and grounded in a highly inclusive and educated sort of seeing or looking. Such look-see, turned on language in use, is the vision not only of linguistic activities, but also shows us what to think and say about all activities that are characteristically human. This is because our language stylizes and colors them all. For example, we can laugh and weep because we can speak. No sub-human animal can dine or take a walk, though he can eat and move. A mountain goat can leap from ledge to ledge, but it cannot go mountain climbing like sportsmen who can talk. So Austin, for example, has asserted that we had better think of philosophy practiced this way as "phenomenology," since we now think of the phenomenologist as the sensitive seer of anything in its conceptually unspoiled nature. This has resulted in the curious notion of "philosophy beyond philosophy-as-formulated," which has currency now in various areas and which perhaps I'll want to say much more about later. The final remark for the nonce in this connection is reminiscent of Merleau-Ponty, the greatest of the French phenomenologists: all consciousness is perceptual—not conceptual—in fundamental intention. Anyway, this is specially true of my rapport with things. I look and see and get an impression. Philosophical *concepts* may or may not come, after that. And incidentally.

This is why I must now, in my latter years, turn to a style of writing that is full of immediacy, to convey the quality of my philosophical experience. This is to assume that there is such a thing as *experience* which is philosophical, a moot point needing more incubation to show what is in it. For me, then, being philosophical is not merely, or even mainly, an affair of acquiring well-formed concepts. A literary form such as that of the short story might therefore be more to my purpose. I'm not going to hesitate to use it in tid-bits whenever I feel the need, out of a spontaneous approach. Like Orlando, I can live no longer by just thinking. Rather, by imaginative participation.

But why should looking back at what I have lived through in my century make me sad? Partly it is the import of what has happened to the whole world, in various dimensions, especially in technology and in the theater of socio-political thought and action. I'll want short stories on that, in the literary vein. But there is a more personal reason. My own person or my own life has always been a vacuous sort of nonentity, in itself. There seems to be nothing about myself in particular for me to remember when I look back. It is as if what I have been is an empty place which has been occasionally filled with the lives of other people. Not my own life. Even they have found nothing positive in me. But, in the hollow that I am, they have been activated and nourished, while I remained as nothing, a catalyst. How well I understand the existentialist talk about Nothing, and Hegel's *Negativität* (principle of negation), and the mystic's Nirvana!

But I have had wonderful impressions, too good for me to sense them as just *mine*. It is these that I simply must salvage, for they have come to me, not as parts of me marking *my* identity, but as goods intended for others whom I must help to possess them. I've been in current philosophy long enough to know that "your having my impression" is a tricky phrase, usually rubbing the logic of impression-terms up the wrong way. But I've just said that the impressions I must convey are not strictly mine. They are to be "seen" or had by you too, if I can sensitize you by the right line of suggestive talk. If I fail in this task, I shall be guilty of betrayal of cosmic trust. But don't get too comfortable over the prospect of being exposed to impressions only. I am going at times to take the impression apart, with a loving ferocity that grinds small, partly out of diabolical delight in annoying pompous people with fine analysis, partly as an expression of the silent despair my own failings have generated from the beginning.

Once a professor who, having failed to realize in writing his intense inner life of philosophical ferment, resigned from teaching and became the flower gardener on a rich old lady's estate. The flowers grew as if by magic. But it was not magic. All day the gardener—the philosopher *manqué*—was at his job, late into every night he studied in books the ways of flowers. He grew thinner, sadder, and wiser as things burgeoned around him. They grew in the hollow of his living death. Thus was he proving something to Nature. Each season was a step in his demonstration to Nature of how good he could have been as a philosopher if She had really used him for the job She had assigned him in the first place. Now it was a resentment welling up from the foundations of the world that was moving him to grow beautiful flowers that won prizes in the exhibits. One day the little dowager lady said to him affectionately, "How you must love flowers!" His look became distant as he muttered "Damn you!" "What was that?" she said, stiffening. "Pardon me," he said, "I was not addressing you," and this time he stooped to pull up a fledgling larkspur by the roots and leave it exposed to die in the sun.

2.

About technological developments in my time and my remark that it makes me sad to think of them. This by itself is very misleading. I love a fine machine and a delicate instrument animated by light and electricity into performing miracles. Surely nobody can naturally hate such things. The people who reject them do so under the spell of a false philosophy, an unnatural one. Like Gandhi. This reminds me of India. I was born of missionary parents in central India, with tigers and sinners around. My father enjoyed saving the souls of the sinners partly because this involved riding to and fro in the temperamental contraptions that in those days had red hot exhaust pipes that the floor board did not quite cover, vehicles that would burn out their bearings at, for my father, a gratifying rate. When this happened on a trip, he would steer the pounding thing's front end up on to an irrigation ditch, pull the oil pan, and insert a new bearing. For him, the operation of putting the car in condition to continue the journey to its destination fused with the other operation of setting the benighted Hindu soul on the path to its true destiny. Both were for him in response to his calling, and I shared the experience as a little boy beside him on the dusty road. I have now the fifteen-year-old Chevrolet, a 1950 model, that he left me at his death in retirement in Iowa. When I got it four years ago it was in absolutely perfect condition, despite its age of ten years. Now it is a bit rusty around the edges but it still looks new from a few paces back. Strangers have approached me and offered to buy it from under me. Lest I make myself look more like a sentimental lover of antiques than I am, I should confess that I have an eight-year-old Buick which I prefer for longer trips. But it too is getting loving care, and I shall keep it until pressured into buying a newer used car, which will offend me like all the others at first, until I have had time to get acquainted with its ways and sympathize with them. Such sympathy, I have noticed, has acted like an ectoplasmic lubricant for the moving parts of my cars, reducing friction and making them want to continue longer in the service that is perfect freedom from wear and tear. You will say this is a picturesque and animistic way of talking about the cars I have loved. Well, yes, but there is a lower and a higher animism. What I have said can be put in terms of the higher animistic philosophy, in which sense my description is objectively true. But we are going to have to watch that word "objective" since it is a tricky one with various uses. I am simply bulging with things to be said on that score, some of them rather technical.

    Such early experiences of cars on the road converted me to a curious sort of polytheism. They revealed to me that a road is a god. Remember Aristotle's description of God as the Unmoved Mover? Well, remove the capitals and see how nicely the description fits a road. Pluralize Aristotle's monolithic concept a bit and you have a notion that applies to roads. Without itself moving, a road moves you. You move lovingly in response to empty highways crying, "Who'll beyond the hills away?" as Housman said. A little anxiously too, because life is so short and the essence of death is immobility. Now or never. Such journeyings properly made are little pilgrim's progresses during which destination and destiny coalesce as, in the mountain climber's experience, the arrival at the summit is both a reaching his destination and a fulfilling of his destiny as a sportsman. Unfortunately, driving a car is not this sort of experience for many people because it is not a sport for them. This means that there is no exaltation in it, as there would not be in mountain climbing for them. Such games demand precision and coordination without which the situation is dangerous, but with which it is safe, or safe enough. Where there is no risk deliberately incurred and mastered under rules, there is no game, no sport. And the greater the risk to life itself, artfully mastered, the more expressive of the human condition the game. Of course, the people who hug life, the life-huggers, will not understand all this. Their primary concern is security and insurance policies in which they become immobilized. You can go on existing that way for quite a while. To be ultimately safe in this sense is to be dead. Since he makes no mistakes, a dead man has no accidents. But neither does he know anything of the zest of the characteristically human activities that define being alive as a man.

Housman's poetic reference to highways is now unfortunate. Roads would have been better. "Highways" at present suggests expressways and turnpikes. If driving a car is to have the quality I am celebrating, it must be permitted a spontaneity and a closeness to other human goings-on. The driver must be allowed occasional bursts of speed, and the feel of the road as he winds more slowly by places where people live, and the privilege of stopping where he wills for a chat with a stranger at a food or drink counter. His car, serving him this way, is more intimately a part of his very body. This is the way to abridge the difference between riding with your wheels and walking with your legs. The wheels are then as much yours as are your legs; driving a car is not the profoundly expressive sport it is capable of being without such incorporation.

On the turnpike he is denied all this. The entrances and the exits are dictated. You feel regimented. Once on, you get dictated to right down the line. *You* never stop by the way, not even for repairs. It is the *car* that stops if it breaks down. You then are angry with it as you look anxiously forward and backward to see if some suspicious patrolman is approaching with a reprimand. Your own car in these circumstances is not a part of you; it is a foreign body. When it needs repair by a country roadside, it is as if a part of you is in pain and you amble off to one side to give it sympathetic care. Also, you tend not to view the land and the life flanking the expressway because they are so remote from it. It by-passes them. So you get sleepy as you drive with a glazed frontward look that gets glassier hour by hour. You are no longer rolling on *your* wheels as you walk with your legs, walking is a wakeful exercise. You cannot go to sleep as you walk. Neither will you be sleepy if you are really driving down a real road, with a feel for the life on both sides and the sustaining land beneath.

A well-known philosopher recently said that present-day Anglo-American philosophers have gotten off the highway of philosophy where traditionally they belong. He is a traditional philosopher so he has vitriolic things to say about philosophers wandering along the by-ways that for us are the winding blacktop roads close to plain people and their abodes. He meant the philosophers of language. The dominant trend among these at present is indeed to do as much imaginative and sympathetic justice as possible to the language that people live by. They are taking close-up looks at the informal logic of expressions that have to do with non-special experience, in the various situations of life as any man lives it. It is this pursuit that, during the last thirty years or so, has drawn the new philosophers of language off the traditional highway of philosophy into the by-ways where people live. They are now doing what is best called the phenomenology of language.

But beginning some fifteen years before that period, even philosophy of language was practised in a way that kept it on the turnpike of traditional philosophy. This means that it was systematic and formal. The concern then was to construct artificial and ideally perfect languages in the abstract. Perfect, that is, for the purpose of some special discipline such as science. This was then taken as the model for any meaningful and respectable bit of human discourse. As Bridgman said, showing his commitment to the operationally defined concepts of physics, the time would come when people at lunch would have less to say, because they would have no use for the conversational chatter which at present passes for significant talk. The logical positivists, Carnap for example, formalized language to exhibit its formal logic, with the scientific model in view for all meaningful talk. This left a large residue of meaningless talk that they admitted was necessary for ordinary human purposes. One doesn't make love, for example, with language controlled by formal logic. So language has an emotive function as well, they said. One may vent his feelings with words, and it is natural to need to do this on occasion. But, strictly, language is meaningless when functioning this way. Just as frown doesn't have "a meaning" but rather exhibits a feeling of dislike, so does the linguistic expression, "You shouldn't have done that!" Thus language may be used to save the speaker the fatigue of facial exercise, since it functions expressively in exactly the same way in the emotive cases. Polite manners sometimes require the linguistic expression instead of the more impulsive wordless exhibition. In so far as even poetry and metaphysics and religion have any use, it is of this emotive sort only. They contain no true or false assertions of any matters of fact. So said the logical positivists.

But it was the great metaphysical systems in the earlier history of philosophy that were on the true highway of speculative thought, according to the critical fellow who denounced its being now lost on the by-ways. However, even in those cases, the premium was on formal commitments to first principles and logically ordered procedure from them. The metaphysician got on to this turnpike by espousing some grand thesis, like materialism or its opposite spiritualism, or rationalism opposing empiricism, and then he had to stay on it till the next exit twenty deductive steps away, at which point he would pause for a look at things around him with the air of getting some inductive support (nurture) for the rigidly controlled intellectual excursion. At such points he would, of course and incidentally, eat a hot-dog, answer a call of nature, and relax into a trivial exchange with someone who lived there. (Hume slipped in a game of backgammon to keep himself sane as a plain man, Bentham played pushpin, the game of darts.) Then back on to the expressway abstracted from and by-passing the life on both sides, until the traveler needed again to stop, and stand on good earth.

Our scowling critic was indeed right about present-day philosophers having gotten off the turnpike of systematic thought. But they had good reasons, one being that philosophizing should be closer to living. The existentialists have done this in one way, the Anglo-American language philosophers in another. At present, the new phenomenologists are seeing and saying things that promise to reconcile the differences between these philosophers who have strayed off the turnpike to linger with things in a more intimate encounter. I shall want a closer picture of this development sooner or later.

3.

It dawns more and more clearly on me, the longer I reflect on it, that scientific technology at present is placing us without options on limited access highways, with blatant signs all along dictating how and where one is to proceed. In this respect, we used to be closer to vitalizing and individuating things and activities than we are now. Willy-nilly, human destiny is being reduced to destination. This point of arrival is determined by the direction of technological developments, not by Tom or Dick or Harry even if they are the technologists. In my time, I have noticed how such a destination has had to be pictured and praised in more and more strident and glowing terms because there is less and less glow or exaltation in the present journey towards it. We must suffer the temporary dehumanization necessary to getting to the Utopian end, we are told. I am thinking particularly of the Communist ideology and practice. The Communist is the fiercest technologist, so he has to be the loudest in his emphasis on how humanly good the end will be. Something like this note is being sounded more and more here in my beloved country, as the pressure for technological achievement grows and the collectivized consciousness with it. This notion of the good-of-all-in-the-end, under the spell of technological advance, is the host on which the notion of the welfare state has become parasitic. Ortega y Gasset says that a certain dehumanization is necessary to good art. Now there are many who say that this is necessary to good society.

Curiously, the trend in philosophy has been the reverse of this. In my time, in fact only in the last thirty five years of it, philosophy has gradually become the conscience of people grieved by any wholesale thinking that tends to dehumanize men by strident generalizations which make a great and beautiful variety of unique things look like a single big one. Philosophy *began* by taking on expressway forms that could serve ideological purposes. Perhaps the new phenomenology that is now emerging is both a protest to that, and to the regimented "people's democracy" that technological pressures threaten us with at present. It is trying to be *Lebensphilosophie* now, in a new way. It wants now to be an adequate expression of the humane in life, while itself being one of the most humane activities, trying to recognize subtle controls that preserve and even define sanity of human thought and action. There is a new humanism in current philosophy.

Bertrand Russell has noticed this and, being a philosopher of science and a metaphysician in the old style, has acid things to say about it. He fails to notice the affinity between his philosophy and the totalitarian ideology with respect to their tendency to induce science-worship. He is desperately trying to save humanity from the technological know-how that spawns rockets with nuclear warheads, without giving up the principles that subtly underwrite the technological determinism I have been talking about, of which present-day Communism is a clearer cut case than it is of *economic* determinism. It is not the right mode of economic production that will save us now, or the wrong one that is damning us. The crucial thing is to bring to light and apply the right controls on technological know-how, seeing it in the right relations to other forms of human intelligence and activity. Thus a new equalitarianism is needed here that is very different from the current concept of the people's democracy. Insight into this is the supreme good that Spinoza said is as beautiful as it is rare. The people need this sort of shepherd instead of the kind of leader who, according to Castro, demonstrates his greatness by "hurling the masses into conflict," under rockets from Russia. We need a leader who speaks comfortably to us, saying that our warfare is accomplished and showing us how more fully to be men, in the light of a more complete vision of what it is to be a man. Wisdom is nothing if not this.

If this is the need, as indeed it is, I must concede to the turnpike philosophers that the current practice of the by-way philosophers is falling short. But I must say that the new phenomenologists have a closer, and therefore better, view of the human condition we are in, and what to do about it, than the highwaymen who are sniping down at them from the highway. Still, we do need now to move on to a philosophical "synthesis" perhaps of the sort that Ved Mehta only hinted at toward the end of his recent account of British historians, in *The New Yorker*. We need a philosopher—or a group of such—who will do for our age what Aristotle or Aquinas or Kant did for his. Yet with a difference not dreamt of in Mehta's popular view of the matter.

Let me now go a little more precisely and professionally into this matter in the next section.

4.

Anyone who tries to pack the whole of philosophy into a nutshell is going not only to look, but to be, silly in some respects. The result may have some value nevertheless for the general public vaguely disturbed by philosophical questions, if the job is done as well as that kind of thing can be. It could serve even the professionals as a textbook or set of notes for lectures.

The phrase "the whole of philosophy" is ambiguous. This could mean a sort of digest of philosophies that have made their mark in the past or are at present influential. Even this need not be a brief history of philosophy. The issues could be treated systematically or topically, with some mention of the great contributors not in chronological order. This sort of thing has already often been done with a view primarily to the needs of the classroom. But such a work does not present, or argue, a philosophical synthesis.

A synthesis is achieved in such a composition as *The Republic* or Aristotle's *Metaphysics*. This too gives one "the whole of philosophy," but in another sense. It is itself a whole philosophy, as the standard textbook account is not. It is "whole" in spite of the fact that, from the textbookish point of view, it leaves some things out that are philosophically relevant, meaning other philosophical positions each of which may be a whole philosophy. It is whole because you can find in it the philosophy of just about anything you like—love, death, life, dreams, politics, perception, art, religion, science, ultimate reality, and so on. What is relevant to such an enterprise seems to the composer so internal to his "whole philosophy" that the painstaking consideration of other whole philosophies, presented as alternatives on the outside, would be on his part a betrayal, a failure in responsibility to the spirit of philosophy that is moving him. He would tend to turn a deaf ear even to criticisms by others aimed specifically at his work, as does the great artist who composes with a compulsive, consuming, and demonic single-mindedness; like Michelangelo who confessed an inability to understanding his own furiously exclusive dedication to coping in his style with marble. The prevailing image of what goes on in such cases is an erotic one: with the probing chisel the sculptor inseminates the beloved substance and brings the forms in it to birth. Plato said that something like this occurs when the lover of wisdom approaches and "knows" reality, as Adam knew Eve and she conceived and gave birth. A form emerges as the offspring of the act of Platonic love, and gets formulated in the philosophy of the lover.

I call such a philosophy "constructive metaphysics." A philosophical synthesis may be achieved, or be "whole," in this way. Then the model for the interpretation of it will be either a work of art or a plan of living, depending on the prevalence of either a contemplative or a practical aim. This suggestion does not jeopardize its importance or even the possibility of its being true, though "truth" in this use takes some delicate analysis to do it justice, as in art.

One hears wide-spread lamentations these days over the sad decline into which present-day philosophy in the Anglo-American theater has fallen. Where now is a Plato, an Aristotle, a Spinoza, a Kant, a Hegel in that area? In short, where are the lovers of reality? The mourners claim that we need a synthesis for our time, such as those great artists in philosophy provided each for his. The claim is that without such a whole philosophy, we lack an over-all norm for our crucial judgments both of value and fact. It is said that what used to be philosophical intelligence is now disintegrated into picayunish concern with purely logical or linguistic details. Ours has become the age of analysis, whose ultimate concern is the logic, formal and informal, of how we talk; logical positivism on the formal side (Carnap), the "Oxford philosophy" on the informal (Wittgenstein's influence since the middle thirties). The age of prolific coping with the nature of things, spawning constructive metaphysical systems, has passed. Anyway, this is the threnody and the protest, by the people who feel the loss of this cosmic sense of reality.

The Anglo-American philosophers are themselves coming around, at present, to a conception of philosophy that extends it beyond considerations of logic and language, without excluding these. It is not so much that they are modifying their practise; it is, rather, that they are becoming aware of how, as philosophers, they have in fact not been *simply* describing or explicating the uses of expressions. When language is in use, it is in gear with things or circumstances, including constellations of elements that are not proper parts of the language *per se*. Thus an adequate account of the use taxes the imagination, even the dramatic sense, of the philosopher, who must, in this view of philosophy, keep in view the situations in which people live and engage in live talk, and in which they learned the language. Remembering this, and rehearsing the scene of the living use of expressions in the field of his imagination, the philosopher of language will come to realize that such use is an integral and major part of a human being's form of life, shading into the other parts (Wittgenstein). "Form of life" here is a metaphysical concept, but not of "constructive metaphysics." Instead of the monolithic procedure of abstract thought, building a self-consistent system or *Weltanschauung*, a "whole" constructive metaphysics, the aim now is to keep the kaleidoscopic variety of uses and the different criteria and their situations in view, to do justice to all the modes of expression that men live by. This requires keeping a sensitive eye on, a *looking* at, the complex phenomenon of living and dying human beings, instead of turning away from it into *thinking* about it in terms of a formally consistent theory. This emphasis on seeing or looking at the phenomena in all their subtleties as the fundamental *control*, instead of the logic of systematic theory-construction, has recently been called "phenomenological" by a leading philosopher on the Anglo-American side of the fence (J. L. Austin). The aim of this phenomenology of language is to capture and do justice to the most elusive or delicate features of human action in its most distinctive phase, which is linguistic utterance. All the essentially human factors are realized with the help, or in the medium, of language. A man's soul is caught in the texture of his linguistic activities, and there presented for "perception" by the phenomenologist; who then reports what he "sees" in an account the sense of which is too basic to warrant our saying that he is *just* "describing," "analyzing," "explaining," etc., in the specially controlled or distinctive senses of these terms. His investigations are not just "empirical"; that would presuppose a special way of looking ("observation") and a special criterion of sense-making. The reason for this is that "perception," where this is the phenomenologist's look at things, is itself not just empirical observation, or aesthetic insight, or subjective response, or any other special node of experience. It involves a non-special rapport. And it gets reported in the language, not of constructive, but of I shall call "descriptive metaphysics," a synonym for "phenomenology" as I am treating it here.

What about the continental European side of the fence? What conception of philosophy, what judgment of its present condition, have we there?

The answer to this brings out an exciting parallel with what has happened and is happening in the Anglo-American camp. It shows that there is a basic camaraderie with perhaps some invisible handshaking across the fence in the night of basic presuppositions where everything is pretty much in the dark.

The basic and common dissatisfaction is with the formalistic or "rationalistic" models for philosophy. It was first the existentialists who rejected these in favor of *Lebensphilosophie*. Along with this went an impulse to dramatize the human situation in the medium of the verbal representation, and the existentialists have acted on the impulse. So some of their most significant writing is in literary form (Camus, Sartre). Also, some of them are quite conscious of how intimately language and living are interwoven, and what a travesty on language it is to suppose that it needs to be purged, by artificial construction, into a formally precise system of signs (Heidegger).

But the method of existentialism made it into the polar opposite of logical positivism. As the latter was a formal rationalism with no substance, so existentialism developed itself, in opposition to this, as an informal irrationalism, an anti-rationalism with no substance. The existentialist aimed to destroy the constructions of reason or "the mind," and destruction is construction in reverse, its negation. So the existentialist philosophy was left with "Nothing" when it had done its work. Thus it too had to wane with the waning of logical positivism. The metaphysics of existentialism was, in short, a sort of empty constructive metaphysics *malgré soi* like logical positivism, but as its simple and insubstantial negation. Moreover, the existentialists were still in the grip of the old conviction, so characteristic of continental philosophy, that the world and even ordered experience are constructions of thought or will. So if you strip things of the intelligible forms that reason has spun into and around them, which is just what the irrationalist in philosophy does, you will indeed be left with Nothing or Non-Being as the ultimate. There will be nothing left for any sort of perception, or to be looked at in any way, as a control on what the philosopher is to say about the world. Of course, existentialism has much to say, nevertheless, but in a vein either of dramatic expression of chaotic loneliness, or admonition for a desperate will-to-act without any ontological foundation for action.

So, for reasons curiously similar at base to those that undid logical positivism in favor of linguistic phenomenology of the informal sort, existentialism is losing its point and its force as it gives way also to phenomenology, but of a different sort. Instead of emphasizing and studying the pervasive play of language in the field of human experience, the new continental phenomenologists put the emphasis on the non-linguistic phenomena in the field and on forms of consciousness of them, seeking to portray these with the utmost neutrality or without the philosophical preconceptions that philosophers unconsciously employ in constructive-destructive metaphysics. In short, the continental phenomenologists are now also doing what I have called *descriptive* metaphysics and which some of them think of as "metaphysics beyond metaphysics." (Being continentals, they can't help putting it paradoxically.) So now there is a sort of confluence, not yet very explicit, of the continental European with the Anglo-American current of philosophy. Both currents are "phenomenological." It is this meeting of minds that I had in view when I spoke of shaking hands across the fence, in the dark of a basic agreement. The new confluence is rather like another that occurred about two hundred years ago when, on the one hand, the stream of British empirical thought culminating in Hume merged with the current of continental rationalism, in the synthesis of Kant's critical philosophy. Kant also was suspicious of constructive metaphysics—he called it dogmatic—and proceeded to develop a sort of descriptive one which cautiously and carefully developed a consciousness of presuppositions of various sorts of theorizing, scientific, ethical, aesthetic, religious, and metaphysical. A number of present-day phenomenologists are aware of some affiliation of what they are doing with what Kant attempted. Some of them see their own phenomenology as a conciliatory synthesis of existentialism on the one hand and logical positivism on the other.

Because of what "phenomenological" has meant especially in the history of the last hundred and fifty years of German philosophy, the word carries a liability with it. Hegel set the pace for the use of the word that the present phenomenologists are intending to undercut. In his *Phenomenology of Mind*, Hegel went into an orgasmic climax of *constructive* metaphysics, portraying the evolution of the universe as the realization, stage by stage in a necessary succession, of Absolute Mind or Spirit (*Weltgeist*). This did have the merit of giving all the forms of experience and thought their niche in the

Scheme of Things, in an "organic whole." It was a whole philosophy with a vengeance, a philosophy whose main category was "The Whole." The Truth is the Whole (*das Wahre ist das Ganze*).

This is the sort of philosophical synthesis that the new phenomenologists are now shying clear of with distrust and even anxiety. Such a whole philosophy, passionately charged as it is with causes for collective action by national or trans-national groups (Communism), is dangerous. Mass action sparked this way is in principle indistinguishable from the action under the banners of religious crusades or inquisitions. It can be devastating and demonic; indeed, it *tends* to be this, under the leadership of a *Führer* or a Big Brother or a Comrade believing himself, and believed by his passionate followers, to be chosen by the World Spirit—or simply by the Good of Mankind. It is the occasion for the devil, like the dog, to have his day.

So when we say that philosophy now is small, affording no synthesis or world view to live by, we should be careful about the kind of synthesis we are asking for. A philosophical synthesis in some sense we do need, if not always and everywhere of the constructive-metaphysical sort. Can the new phenomenology or descriptive metaphysics give us a philosophical synthesis, and, if so, how will it differ from the constructive sort which more directly addresses itself to, or sparks, a way of life, being more closely akin to ideology?

This is fundamentally a question about philosophical *sanity*, and that is why the answer is delicate and difficult. The people who prefer to live dangerously under the excitement of constructive-metaphysical slogans or ideologies do not want to understand the answer, and therefore will not; they simply must be up and going in favor of The Cause—compulsively, if you want the right psychological term for it. Hegel made the compulsion appear to have a transcendental dimension, *de fond en comble*. I am personally impressed by his metaphysics as a dramatic statement of such compulsion. People do seem to go into trances of concerted action, during which they feel compelled by something cosmic to refuse audience to anyone wanting to investigate the fundamentals objectively, howsoever fair, patient, and neutral the questioner may be in his approach. Maybe men *are* occasionally moved by something of this nature, too deep or high for empirical psychology and sociology to get at, as Hegel believed. It is perhaps better understood in a philosophical vision such as is afforded by his own constructive metaphysics of the mainsprings of human action. But if such a view as this is true in any sense at all, there is need for an opposition to it—philosophy that keeps the human theater of thought and action as sane as possible by psychically distancing people from mainsprings of massive action that can be deadly if allowed the full measure of passion prescribed by philosophical ideologies such as Hegelianism used for political ends, as by fascism and communism. The threat of this in our day is immense. I suggest that the new phenomenology that is now quietly crystallizing as our philosophical conscience is in answer to this menace, either in opposition to it or at least as a control on this demonic ingredient of human nature—even of "reality" if you accept the *Weltanschauung* of the unleashed metaphysical imagination. Not that the new phenomenological consciousness tends to paralyze human action, or, on the other hand, to prescribe forms of it. Rather, it considers the sort of action in question, its motivation and rationale, in distinction from alternatives alongside it as feasible options. So it is more pluralistic than the *wholesale* procedure of the ideological sort of constructive metaphysics that it discourages.

What I have been saying can be illustrated as follows:

(a) logical positivism ——————— (b) existentialism
(c) the new phenomenology——— (d) constructive metaphysics
                                          (mainly ideological)

This shows that the new phenomenology (c) is a synthesis of logical positivism and existentialism, while itself standing out *in opposition to* constructive metaphysics, especially of the ideological sort. This is the present condition of philosophy, at least in the Occident. I make this remark as a historian of philosophy. The *next* synthesis, not yet achieved in any well worked out way, will fuse (c) and (d) in a coherent "whole" philosophy. This makes it look as if the present-day phenomenology, itself still in a formative stage, is not the last word. Well, I for one cannot help considering it under that limitation. This does not bother me because, as I see it, there is a sort of virtue in formulating a philosophical theory tidily enough for later philosophers to detect its limitations, and for it thus to be superseded. I distrust a philosophy so perennial and so vaguely couched that it accommodates just about any judgment, such that it may be espoused at any time by some and rejected by others, for reasons outside, or not relevant to, the validity of the philosophy in question. Hegel's philosophy is an example, seeming to say everything or nothing, according as it is believed or disbelieved; these alternatives being optional. Such a "whole" philosophy therefore serves us, and perhaps should be judged, as a work of art if the mood is contemplative, or as a spur to grand action, right or wrong, if the mood is practical.

But what of the constructive metaphysics which is not "mainly ideological"? *Are* there not such philosophies? The answer is affirmative, and brings out the necessity of recognizing degrees of "ideological." For example, Platonism and Aristotelianism are primarily occasions for coherent or "whole" contemplative visions of the nature of things; their bearing on, and regulation for, a way of life is a secondary, yet important, part of their significance. If you are an Augustine (Platonism) or an Aquinas (Aristotelianism) you will put the philosophy into working relation with a religious way of life. This would be to interpret it ideologically, with the resulting organization for concerted action, under high leadership. To preserve sanity here too, in the religious cases, understanding is needed and the new phenomenology is concerned about this also, seeking for a fair recognition of the "logic" of the language and practices of religion. Understanding this will provide the controls.

Some constructive metaphysics seems even farther away from ideology. Such cases do little more than illuminate for intellectual vision what is "ultimately real." That is, it is hard to give them an ideological application in favor of a certain way of life. I think for example of Whitehead's philosophy of organism and process, or of Santayana's metaphysics of scepticism and animal faith. Though both these philosophies show traces of eclecticism, each is certainly a whole philosophy and a case of constructive metaphysics. Yet no one has given either of them a flamboyant ideological interpretation to galvanize people into concerted action. The new phenomenology is not so much opposed to such contemplative metaphysical constructions as it is concerned to get at the principles of understanding them. And it does not itself do philosophy in this constructive way that provides occasions for great philosophical visions. It is committed to descriptive metaphysics, a philosophy that ideally will be "whole," but not with the wholeness and coherence that one has in view when considering a work of art, or a plan or a set of instructions for a comprehensive and complete action. The wholeness that the new phenomenologist aims at will be clarified in later portions of the philosophical reflections we are engaged in here.

What this phenomenology is more pointedly *opposed* to is perhaps best brought out by considering what is *causing* it, in a broad cultural context. (So the question of what *justifies* it will be *another* question.) The new phenomenology is at present emerging in answer to a need for a curb on massive action and the kind of ideological thinking that sparks it. It is a sedative for the social organism that tends to act insanely under the influence of the ideology. Or, since the patient does not permit such sedation as a rule, phenomenological considerations tend more to provide a ballast for individuals and societies that need to protect themselves against the contagion of such insanity of thought and action. This makes it, in its present form, the metaphysics of democracy. But it is important to notice that this is true only if democracy is construed as a form of life that is against collective action of *any* sort that is simply dictated by either a minority or a majority. Moreover, and even more important, the descriptive phenomenological consciousness does not as such, or as philosophically formulated, *prescribe* even democratic patterns of action and thought. It serves the democratic way only negatively by *proscribing* what goes on *more conspicuously* on the totalitarian or authoritarian side of the fence. That is, phenomenological considerations *per se* require only a disinterested awareness of the logic of "good reasons" for action of any sort, mental or physical, individual or collective. A grasp of this multidimensional logic is the essence of philosophical understanding, where the latter is purely phenomenological.

What I have been saying is that the new descriptive metaphysics, synthesizing the post-existential, experience-oriented continental philosophy and the post-positivistic, language-oriented Anglo-American philosophy into this new "phenomenology," is anxious—even doubtful—about the importance of being earnest for what this popularly means to socially and politically minded people. It has emerged *in opposition to* the ideological sort of constructive metaphysics which can be used by, say, a Castro "to hurl the masses into conflict." Well, my point is: the spirit of philosophy that assists such mass action takes shape as the ideological sort of constructive metaphysics the menace of which is, culturally speaking, "causing" the new phenomenology to emerge in opposition to it, in answer to the human need for sanity. The phenomenologist in this sense works against odds because vitality seems to be on the side of passionate and demonic action. Hegel said that nothing great was ever achieved without passion, making it look as if this is the way to be "really rational." Such a conviction undercuts the distinction between reason, feeling, and will, and issues in the slogan that true theorizing is *identical* with right practice, where the latter turns out to be the strident collectivized thing demanded by the ideology, overruling "reason" in the dispassionate or impartial sense which the phenomenologist is now concerned to illuminate in a new way, as a solvent for the spell cast by ideologizing. This is what distinguishes the new sense of the word "phenomenology" from the old, such as Hegel's.

This differentiation between constructive and descriptive metaphysics is not here meant to involve a value-judgment in favor of the descriptive, though "sanity" and "insanity" are commonly used as value-terms. But they do have a descriptive use as well, and it is this that has been primary in my thinking about the subject up to this point. The emphasis on the valuational use will come later, and a value-judgment made. However, even now, prior to the careful questions about good-for-what that must be considered before any responsible value-judgment can be made, a casual initial valuation might very properly indicate values on both sides, values of different sorts. There is an ancient and venerable view that profoundly vital values spring from a divine madness as their necessary condition—something beyond dispassionate reason. If this were not the case, religion, art, and even philosophy in some of its forms would not have served us as they have. And it is in view of the disservices of these disciplines when not adequately controlled that sanity with *its* set of values is remembered, the realization and preservation of which is the *special* function of the descriptive metaphysics-for-sanity (the new phenomenology). "Special" here means "important in the present circumstances." The demonic force of current ideological thought-in-action is dangerous to the human spirit; it should have an explicit opposition, and the new phenomenology is emerging to provide it.

In this connection, permit me the following reflection. It can be said that Hegel drained his insanity off into his philosophy, to become its content, leaving his own person sane enough for a successful career of self-promotion. (Think also of Heidegger and Tillich in this light.) It was otherwise with Nietzsche, who failed to objectify his insanity in his trenchant aphorisms. Much of it remained in his own person. This left his works on the whole more intelligible—though more piece-meal—than the murky, ponderous ideology systematically inflated by the method in Hegel's madness. Wittgenstein is more like Nietzsche on this count. Wittgenstein, like his brothers, was close to suicide much of the time; he contained his madness in his person, leaving his written fragments gem-like with suggestions in favor of sanity, more successfully than even Nietzsche who took some viciously exclusive stands against some good things. This whole notion of "objectifying one's madness," whimsically presented here, has clinical and aesthetic overtones, like Aristotle's concept of *catharsis*. You can save yourself from a psychological disturbance by objectifying it in an expressive formulation, dramatic or otherwise; and you will then be at the psychical distance from it necessary to aesthetic contemplation. But, while this may save *you*, the composition will tempt others to appropriate it as a risky instrument of insane action, if their genius is practical and if language is the medium of the composition—a bit of constructive metaphysics, an ideology.

So again, from another angle, we reach the conclusion that the notion of "a philosophical synthesis" is too broad to warrant the judgment that it is always needed, without qualification. Not only is the consideration of the *kind* of philosophical synthesis always important, with a view to circumstances, but sometimes the primary need will be not for another synthesis of *any* sort, but rather for philosophical analysis, historically speaking or again with a view to circumstances. The history of philosophy amply illustrates this. For example, the concrete practical and ethical needs, and the "common sense," of the ancient Greeks were better satisfied by a critical and disintegrative, even sceptical, analysis of the constructive metaphysics of Plato and Aristotle that tended to, after the "metaphysical period" of magnificent systems of thought about ultimate reality. So there emerged the "ethical period" of more specific and individual concerns, an early age of practical analysis. This was like Hume's later reaction to Descartes' metaphysics of ultimate certainties about God and the cosmos, though here the analysis was more concerned with details of the theory of knowledge and perception than with ethics.

The analogue to this in our own age of analysis, at mid-twentieth century, is the careful consideration of the logic of modes of expression, or of the "language" of science, art, morals, religion, which is the emphasis in the Anglo-American theater. On the continental European side, the stress is on the way of looking or mode of perception that undergirds or grounds the mode of expression in question.

This pursuit of "presuppositions" of experience and expression is perhaps "analytical" in some large or vague sense of the term. These so-called analysts are themselves unhappy about the unfitness of the term in any precise sense in application to the way they are doing philosophy. This is why some of them, Austin for example, explicitly reject "analytical" in favor of "phenomenological" as the right adjective, though he [Austin] is worried about its being such a "mouthful."

5.

Now, I again take up the thread of my impressions of technology. The way in which Gandhi and, say, the southern agrarians with headquarters at Vanderbilt were wrong about technology is hard to say. But they were wrong. I don't want to dwell on this difficult point. The long and short of what is wrong about it is that technological intelligence was already at work in the production and use of bows and arrows and wooden plows and wheels. No sub-human animal does anything like this. Not even the beaver building the dam or the bird building the nest. They simply use what nature has produced. When Congo, the chimpanzee, takes to finger-doodling with paint on canvas, it is not engaged in the human action called painting because it is congenitally incapable of producing either the paint or the canvas. Man is the artifact-producing animal, and sling-shots and ox-carts and paint are artifacts. If you sanction these, you approve of technology and, in principle, anything it can make, including thermonuclear devices and rocket-ships. At some point in the development you may properly say that a certain product tempts people to uses of it that fail to serve the purpose—the hydrogen bomb for fighting a war to be survived and won, the space-ship to take you where you need to go. But, having approved of arrows and ox-carts, you cannot consistently or even wisely say wholesale that technological intelligence is to blame for the evils of mankind. I say not even wisely because putting the lid on technological advance in an otherwise civilized society tends to result in tumescent pseudo-developments in religion and art, something not true to the spirit of man, either as a whole or to his special capabilities. Then art and religion have to take over the functions of science, in pseudo-practices that are neither here nor there. (By the same token, a society that suppresses the religious function in favor of the scientific, as in Communist countries, confers upon its art and technology an ideological control which is its camouflaged way of continuing to be religious, thus again denaturing all three functions into a potpourri of pseudo-activities.)

Perhaps the formula that Gandhi had obliquely in mind, and therefore not very clearly, could be put somewhat as follows: don't let technological achievements de-activate any fundamental human faculty as, just for example, the linguistic. Consider television, to illustrate the point.

Television is for adults only. Children who have been exposed to it from infancy suffer from an insufficient exercise of their own imagination. The point is not at all that they have been subjected thereby to poor use of the language. This happens just as much to children who have had only radios to listen to. But even the latter have an important advantage. Children must more thoroughly learn the language if the story told in words-without-ready-made-pictures is to be got with all its dramatic force. In short, their own imagination is activated to supply the spectacle, via the language. As a result, their use of the language and their thinking in its terms become more imaginative as they mature. The teacher who has been teaching for twenty years or more notices that he now has to find methods of conveying what he has to say to students without relying on a certain spontaneity of the student imagination in response. There is not now as much pictorial blossoming of the sense of his remarks into the sort of resilient understanding on the part of the student that presents him with an idea to be dwelt on and detailed on his own power, after the teacher has had his say. Television has been that sort of bleach for about fifteen years now, and college teachers are beginning to sense it.

It goes without saying that for some purposes a television set serves us better than a radio, better even than the teacher in person. And if the televised picture is already the fruit of a fine imagination, beyond the capacity of the young learner's imagination to produce unaided, let the child be exposed to it by all means. It is only the leprosy of the imagination, contracted by people who have been prevented by pictorial spoon-feeding from learning to use language for all it is worth, that I am protesting. And the triumphs of technology that do this sort of thing to people are to be watched with special suspicion. Man is, in essence, a language-using animal. This definition is much more to the point than Aristotle's to the effect that man is a rational animal. The essential dehumanization is the one that impairs a man's ability to do the many wonderful things that can be done with language, of which thinking rationally is only one.

My protest is not sentimental, but unfortunately it is inadequately worked out. The following final impression about this whole problem is also vague, yet quite important. It goes like this: as television curtails imagining some good things, so the atom bomb curtails fighting for some good things. And as the radio is better on the first count, so is the rifle on the second. With a rifle, it is the soldier who does the fighting; as with a radio it is the listener who does the imagining. And a man as a man needs to do one or the other or both, upon occasion. Atomic weapons are now either frightening him from his military duty—think of Hungary and Cuba—the alternative to doing nothing being participation in a rash action of total devastation that no longer has the quality of fighting. Engaged in that, you are not a man of war. The days of noble warriors are over. The situation is such that you are either a rash man or a coward, the Aristotelian mean of true courage being no longer a feasible alternative. So, if Aristotle is right—he usually is on such matters—you are committed to the vice of excess or the opposite one of deficiency, thanks to atomic weapons. Rocket rattling is one thing, a non-human clatter. Sabre rattling is bad but it is a human action.

I speak as if fighting is not only a human but a humane action. It certainly is both these in some situations, even with a rifle and marksmanship that put out of commission a brute force bent on destruction of a good thing and that cannot be stopped by other less deadly means available then and there. Also, a fine rifle is just right for the excellent sport of hunting, another very human action. But I realize that such remarks open the flood gates to ponderous arguments pro and con. Sometimes the best way to put an end to them is to get naughty and candid like the woman hunter of African big game whose title for an essay justifying hunting was, "I Just Love to Kill Things." Under rules of the sport, to be sure, if it is to be expressive of anything in Nature. In short, if it is to be a humane and not a cruel activity.

6.

Here are two stories about technology, suggested by Renoir's exclamation, "This earth, paradise of gods!" They express a theology for artists.

At first the invisible gods were scattered through the universe. Each was very alone in that vast and dark distribution. One by one they discovered the earth with its thin layer of warm, moist air lavendered by the light of the sun and the fragrance of growth. Here there was color and color-space. The gods loved the place and the company, so they made it their abode, forming a happy though solemn assembly of spirits animating the earth. All things there became full of gods. Before, in their primordial condition of being lost in empty space, the distinction between life and death had not been realized, not even by the gods. Then, on the earth, it became clear cut. The gods loved this, but their presence in things made the earth a little sad and anxious with the reminder of how closely intermingled living and dying are, fundamentally. This is what made things beautiful. Thus did an echo of the primordial condition get embodied in the world, and the gods became its meaning.

After a while the good earth became fertile with the birth-pangs of imitation of the gods animating it, and men began to grow out of it. The gods enjoyed this new company too at first. Men were so like them, with loves and ultimate loneliness that, one after another, would animate the colors in the sky.

But men, unlike the gods, had chemicals in their systems and this eventually showed in a pervasive consciousness of the chemistry of things. All things became full of just chemicals, for men. They even saw each other this way, and proceeded to act accordingly toward their environment including each other. Everything became a physical stimulus-response mechanism. An intoxicating power to transform nature and human nature developed along with this consciousness, which blinded them to the presence of the gods. They began to spray pesticides from the drab sky that had been so full of color. So the gods met in solemn assembly and decided that man must be evicted from the garden of the earth, the paradise of gods. Having himself become a pest he must be annihilated. The best way to do this would be to augment his technological know-how till it produced for him the hydrogen bomb. Thus did the gods let man choose the weapon for the final cosmic duel, the weapon by which he was to be removed from the scarred face of the earth, leaving it again in a space full of color and the meaning of life-and-death.

The second story reads like the first up to the point where the troubled gods meet to decide man's fate. Then it goes on as follows:

The gods looked at one another and remembered that it was at first by imitation of them that men had come into being. They too, the eternal gods, had known not only love and loneliness but also the conflict and ambition that love so spontaneously generates. So they still loved men and resolved somehow to save them. "The diagnosis of man's ailment showed that he had become unto himself a barren land, a soulless creature, because of the blight of the chemical consciousness of things. But it also revealed that this way of looking at and conceiving things was an integral part of human nature. The gods therefore decided to save man's soul by frightening him out of the excesses of his technological intelligence. They would give him the thermonuclear bomb. This would preside as the real chairman at peace-council tables, preserving the peace through fear of atomic conflict. The bigger the bomb for this purpose, the better. Not one hundred but two hundred megatons. Who could really fight with that? Eventually this artificial cowardliness and the shame over it would move men to round out their true natures with an ancient wisdom. Men again would be whole, and they would see again that all things are full of gods. Thus did the gods plan to save mankind.

Which story is true? Or truer if you want degrees of truth? The stories and the question are whimsical, but if you take them seriously, including the question, you will run into the sort of logical questions about the language of religion and its confirmation that bedevil anyone concerned about the truth of any religion. I defy anyone "simply" to show that the stories are false. Each is a most excellent myth, though not a living or gripping one because it is contrived, unlike the world myths that have mushroomed out of prereflective depths, in a language that masters and moulds men instead of being mastered and moulded by them. Moreover, it would not do to maintain that they are nothing but stories with morals, though a moral can be teased out of each. In another legitimate though subtle interpretation they are not just stories but histories, true in a way that I want to clarify under the right auspices. The approach to that problem will have to be right if I am to communicate anything like my impression of the solution.

But I was meditating on nuclear weapons. Strictly, there are no nuclear warheads because you can't go really warring with them, where this means the action of fighting that men must occasionally engage in even as men, not brutes or robots. But I've finished making that point. My point now is that Bertie Russell and the like-minded people who put on mass demonstrations against destruction by atoms would help their cause mightily if they made it even clearer than some of them have that they are not just pacifists, and if they refused to let the latter band up with them in demonstrations. Straight pacifism is a muddled and soft headed philosophy of what it is to be a man. Or a god. God without thunder—remember John Crowe Ransom's book with that title—falls short both of divinity and reality. You can't explain anything that goes on in human affairs or elsewhere with a god whose lightning never kills anything. The pacifist who is wholly against taking any human action that involves killing, never mind the circumstances, is paralyzed either by a sentimental dream of "noble savages" in a past Golden Age or a no less false vision of the Utopia that would descend on us at present were we to stop fighting and killing. He fails to notice the refined cruelty in the demand that such pacifism makes. I don't mean the cruelty to others whom he refuses to protect because of the demand that immobilizes him, though this is bad enough. The essential cruelty is wrought upon the immobilized pacifist himself. The ultimate violence is done to him by his pacifism. The others, whom he is not permitted to save by taking natural protective action, die a natural death. He dies an unnatural one as he stands by and watches. Were they to come to life again, they might forgive him, realizing that there was a curious sort of self-sacrifice with a vengeance in the stand he took. But the pacifist who survives the self-mutilation and unnatural death inflicted on him by his wholesale pacifism usually comes out of it with an implacable hatred of it for having betrayed his manhood, especially where the circumstances press him long and hard. He then rages ever after against the dying of the light that he permitted to go out.

People, good people, sense all this, which is why pacifists vex them. They are against pacifism while being whole-heartedly for many good things, including peace. It is because they vigorously love these that they can fight with a clear conscience unmuddied by strange and perplexing beliefs. So I say that the anti-atom demonstrators should be more discriminating, closing their ranks against the anti-war pacifists instead of collaborating with them. The pacifist is against the atomic weapon because he is against war. I am against such weapons because their availability makes warring problematic when it is required. And required it sometimes certainly is.

I may have given the impression that I like war, since I have spoken of noble warriors and described genuine warfare as a significant human activity. Also, my reason for decrying atomic weapons was that it makes real fighting impossible. I have made it look as if telling a man he must abstain in all circumstances from lethal fighting is like telling him he mustn't use language with poetic license since the scientific use is the ideal. And this, some people will say, is unfair. Preventing a man from fighting that involves killing is not like prohibiting an action that is necessary to his human condition, like poetizing. Moreover, some psychologists will analyze my motive as a craven admiration for war produced by my having viewed both world wars from a psychical distance. I was a little too young to participate in the first one, and a little too old for the second. This, the Bullough-minded psychologists will say, has put war also at a psychic distance in my view of it and made it look beautiful. So here I am wishing war on everybody, as a grand expression of human nature. Someone will also, at this point, remind me of my lust for hunting and killing animals with a "fine rifle." Thus will I be psycho-analyzed into a quasi-sadist for whom the painful (masochistic?) self-discipline of pacifism is simply intolerable and doesn't make sense.

Well, the truth is that during the Second World War I had waking nightmares of people shooting and bayoneting people. I simply couldn't believe that these terrible visions of mine, most vivid in the moments just before I really went to sleep at night, were true. Who could instigate and do things like that, I thought, in reality? The horror of it. I was then, in my heart, a pacifist.

The picture that I now have of lethal warfare among people is that, in some circumstances, it is a morally obligatory sort of wrong-doing. This is paradoxical, so I shall want to settle down later to a cluster of meditations on morals, when the main theme is socio-political action. Here it is still technology. The difficulty that I shall have to unsnarl comes out of my saying that, in some situations, it is wrong both to take lethal military action and not to take it, which is indeed a distressing predicament to be in. On the theoretical level, the apparent contradiction must be taken out of it, if not the paradox. Reinhold Niebuhr and Paul Tillich have wrestled with this problem. And with the ethical perfectionism of the pacifists whose alleged solution is too simple.

7.

Very likely war would have broken out here and there in the last two decades since the last world war, had not the atomic threat acted as a deterrent. I am thinking of such incidents as Hungary and Suez and Lebanon, more conspicuously Cuba. Without the rocket threat from Russia, the enslavement of Cuban minds by Communist ideology could have been averted by a relatively straightforward economic or even military operation. With some assistance, mostly from inside and a little from outside, the Cuban exiles could have been the liberators. But it works the other way too. Fear of atomic holocaust has kept Communist Russia from taking West Berlin. Their ground forces are much superior to those of free Europe.

The point is, however, wouldn't there be more war, sporadic or not, for better or for worse, had there been no rockets to rattle? And shouldn't we therefore love scientific technology *especially* for this invention? My story about the thermonuclear president at peace conferences suggests, whimsically and tentatively, an affirmative answer. If we don't like war, we should like the atomic devices for wholesale devastation that are keeping the peace. The proposition makes me anxious but I am prepared in a way to accept it. Perhaps this *is* the way the gods are going to save us from our chemical selves, giving us pause to remember and cultivate our spiritual needs. Thus the argument for conventional weapons of warfare seems to break down, if not killing innocent people with *any* weapons is a good thing and some good people get killed in almost any war. (The content of that if-clause is certainly true.) What then shall I finally say about the fine rifle?

My answer is delicate and going to be a bit spread out—a gossamer impression that can be easily torn by misunderstanding. I am even going to tempt you to misunderstand it by a teasing and whimsical formulation, in which I protest against a wrong emphasis we have been brought up with. I shall try to straighten this bent stick by bending it the other way, following Aristotle's advice. When I let go, I hope the matter will be straightened out. The gist of my remarks turns on the distinction between persons and things that Kant featured in his famous interpretation of the Christian view of the world. It was Kant's main point that this distinction is ultimate and that only persons are the proper or final objects of moral obligation and love. Things, on the other hand, being mere natural phenomena, are only grist for the technological mill and therefore loving them too as if one has a duty toward them doesn't make sense. Thus a fine rifle or a fine car has an instrumental or market value only and they naturally get cavalier treatment as mere means. It is the pervasive influence of such a doctrine, fortified by the independent snowballing of technological developments, that is at the source of our troubled condition, I believe. The teasing essay on this theme follows, whose title is, if you like, "On Persons as Things."

8.

My dealings with people, and my persistent desire to be kind and just to them, have led me to question Kant's distinction between things and persons and its value in situations calling for moral judgment. The long and short of it is that if I treat people simply as persons, and as rational, and as ends in themselves, I find I am less kind and patient towards then than when I see them also as things. A rational being, with a will free to exercise his reason, may be expected to be reasonable more often than people are. I want to keep rebuking people, to the point of unkindness, when I look upon them only as having free will and the responsibilities of rational agents. Or frequently I simply want to slap them down, as impossible and bad.

No one really wants to slap down a thing. He may occasionally do this if he is tired, but he knows it is silly. I once broke a tennis racket which I was using clumsily, but if I could look on all people all the time as I do on tennis rackets, they would get better treatment from me on the whole, than they do now, thanks to my moral and religious education. I keep expecting conduct, on their part and mine, which is not forthcoming and this angers and depresses me. I brood over flamboyant penalties or become passively sour. A final petulance settles over me and my thoughts about people, in the Kantian view of them as persons.

Suppose, though, I should begin treating people as things. Things are for use, as means to ends, and this would entail using people, which seems harder on them than treating them as ends. Wood is a thing, and you burn it to keep you warm or to cook trout by your tent. And who would want to use people that way? But don't forget that things may be used with love and understanding. That's how most of us use wood for camp fires. Smoke gets in your eyes and you love it, and the wood as it burns. What frightened the Kants in this world was the mistaken image of having to burn people for warmth, so to speak. But that is not what people are good for. They're much better to generate companionship with, and reciprocated love — which, if you like, is a kind of warmth after all. You will use them for this — and yourself for this — when you use them with love and understanding, as you did the wood. The point is that there is nothing intrinsically shocking about using people. It's the way you use them that counts, and to what ends.

Treating people as ends in themselves, never as means, is a vague idea and probably has some merit in some of its interpretations, but not in the Kantian. I find that the ends I have in view when I am behaving decently are never persons as such, but what can be generated by persons getting together, such as companionship and mutual love, as already remarked. Or happiness, if you prefer Aristotle. Happiness is certainly not a person, but it certainly is an end worth respecting with finality. The sensible man entertains an ultimate respect for happiness, but not for persons or personality, except as a means. There probably is no happiness without persons, but this does not equate the two. And it is still the happiness, or some such good, that is to be treated as the end, not the person. Again, the point is that there is a wise way of using persons, as means, including your own person. The ultimate ends are something else, that persons enjoy....

When I broke my tennis racket I felt foolish, the way a parent feels when he thrashes his son or tries to break him for doing wrong. I think all of us parents feel that way about beating children, though we will occasionally do it because we think we have an excuse, in the child's case if not in the racket's.

(There *is* a difference, which I shall recognize presently.) We are taught not to treat the child as a thing like the tennis racket. In the racket's case alone do we feel inexcusably foolish, when we break it for misbehaving.

This is why I wish I had been encouraged from the beginning, to treat persons as things instead of persons. The solution now seems to be to learn to conceive persons as a class of things. Spinoza achieved something like this, so I shall sit for a while at his feet.

For Spinoza, there were only things. He called them modes. To be sure, in the final analysis only one thing existed, namely, Nature or God or Substance, with absolutely no taint of personality. Spinoza had the wisdom to use God as a thing. He was something to love which, for Spinoza, was simply something to understand. God does not reciprocate lovingly, but neither does the wood. Both may serve excellently nevertheless. *You* may love them. The point, however, is that there are modes and these are the more familiar things of our experience. Some modes have the attribute of mind more conspicuously than others, and these are the things we call persons. The *things* that are persons.

What they do, they do for reasons and causes (*i.e.,* compulsions) that stretch way back and run deep. One had better see them in that light. This is the vision that secures for them humane consideration, and gives you peace. Not that you will do nothing about anything. You, or nature through you, will use them as feelingful and thoughtful things, to share with them as much love and companionship as possible. The love of God (the understanding of things, *i.e.*) is the general condition to be satisfied, if these goods are to be realized. We use wood for warmth and shelter, and persons to generate the warmth and light of friendship and the shelter of love.

There is a sense in which a child, not a tennis racket, does things on its own hook. It has initiative, as we say, or choice. It is an agent in a way in which wood, in the form of a racket, is not. Only a short-lived view would deny this plain fact. So if, like Spinoza, we are going to call people things without committing ourselves to this silly denial, we must repeat that there are different classes of things. It is proper, in fact morally obligatory, to consider the class known as people as free things, provided you mean that they are responsive to kinds of motives to which sub-human things can't respond. I reason with my son, not with my racket. Reasons don't move the racket. Only causes do. Reasons, with their pivots in the past and future and in possibilities, move me to move my son by exposure to those reasons. If they move my tennis racket at all, it is through me. Not directly the racket. So it is not free, and I am. But I am still a thing, the sort occasionally moved by reasons. I belong, as do people, to the class of rational things—thinking things if you want Descartes' term without his special concept. When I view myself and others this way, I will reason with myself and them, and sense the vast entourage of determining reasons (and causes) only a few of which are there for explicit notice. The rest is silence—with great motive power nevertheless. In this view of you as a thing, I shall understand why *my* reasons are often not dominant in your behavior. I shall, to our mutual advantage, understand you philosophically, which is to be aware of the wide system of motives without being aware of all the components. I like this conception of philosophical understanding. Besides distinguishing it from the scientific, it has the virtue of stressing what earmarks wisdom. The philosopher or seer, in this light, is one whose conduct is determined by this massive insight. Some people are philosophical congenitally, without much if any explicit formulation of a philosophy. They are moved unawares by that cosmic sense. This gives them the necessary ballast for peaceful and friendly living—the life of reason in the meatiest sense of the term. Not all professional philosophers are philosophical. Comparatively few of them have the wise, civilizing thing-view of people. So they too are disturbed by consuming flurries of passion. They see people only as persons and as ends, never to be treated as means and as things.

Since friendship, spontaneous and free, is what people are mainly good for, if they begin failing you systematically on that score, you simply remove them, like a misfitting shoe that chafes irremediably or the dust which Jesus told the disciples to wipe off after they had been in an unfriendly place. The wisdom and morality of such treatment of people, as chafing things, is even more obvious when a way of life that on principle prohibits friendly, spontaneous meeting of minds seizes them. They then collectively become a menace and must be disposed of, like the shoe that hurts. This sometimes means war. But, even then, since we are treating them like misfitting things, we needn't be consumed with hatred as we fight, another excellent point that Spinoza drove home. There is never any occasion for passionate blaming, on the thing-view of people.

We simply take firm and intelligent action. There is a kind of Trash Pile in nature on which all incorrigible misfits eventually land, as nature takes its course. Nature moves us to help her put the trash where it belongs. . . .

So ends the little essay. It may seem right away to favor the Communist view of individual human beings as mere means to a collective end. It seems to sanction the practice that liquidates them if they get in the way. But that is the wrong impression to get of the essay. The whole point is that things, whether they are persons or not, are to be loved each for its own sake, and that there is an affectionate use of things as of persons. The suggestion is that people who are disinclined or impotent to love non-personal things turn out to be pallid lovers even of persons. The two loves go together since they stem from the same deep potency. Unfortunately, it is in just this respect that developments in my century are tending to make us impotent, on both counts. The very invitation to love things is waning, with the consequence that meaningful action expressing love is not so feasible.

How does all this bear on the proposition that there would be more war if we had just fine rifles—

"conventional" weapons—to fight with? At this point I remember George Bernard Shaw's sarcastic remark, made before atomic weapons appeared, to the effect that at solemn peace councils the nations are deliberating whether to kill one another with eighteen inch guns or, in more gentlemanly fashion, with sixteen inch guns. This puts the concept of conventional weapons on the spot and I don't want to get bogged down here with that difficulty. My concern is with the general idea that the more the weapon is of the kind that one can incorporate as a part of himself in action as a fighter, the greater the sense of a justification of the lethal action, if the cause is right and the killing necessary to its fulfillment. Then there is room on the battle field for the love that is a tragic understanding of the whole situation, and for this not only to regulate the action but also for the action to be an expression of this ultimate concern, as one fights. One then fights with love and understanding. Spinoza said something like this, and Santayana echoed him afterwards. In short, one who loves things, both animate and inanimate, including the weapon, may be a true warrior when the sad necessity of being one descends upon him. Unlike hunting with a fine rifle, which may be enjoyed as a sport, going to war with one will be a tragic action for the thoughtful man of war, because the enemy, dying of the bullet wound on the field of battle, may exchange confidences with him in language. Remember the key incident in *All Quiet on the Western Front*. Another person is a part of yourself in a special way through the institution of language, so it is as if you die with him. Because of this *special* intimacy between person and person, not holding between person and non-personal thing, a special principle makes it wrong for you to kill a person, even where a sad necessity requires you to. The old paradox again. Sometimes even the genuine hunter's finger is arrested before it pulls the trigger, by such a sense of kinship with the fine specimen that would make a record-breaking trophy, after providing meat for the camp fire and the vesper meditation in the dark mountains that are full of gods. But this sort of sub-linguistic sympathy degenerates into sentimentality if it begins to prevail as an abstract principle. It then becomes the sort of pacifism-in-general that deters a man even from hacking down jungle plants that are between him and a life he wants to save. Albert Schweitzer. He transplants them, en route, and the fellow at the other end dies before he arrives.

9.

Once there was a man who had uneasy feelings about technological developments. One day he read Martin Buber's *I and Thou* which appeared in the German about 1920 and was translated into English some fourteen years later. Buber says very moving things about a personal relation to the world, in which one spontaneously addresses it with help of the second-person pronoun "Thou," This is better even than "God" because a noun may be used in talk *about* what it names, in its absence. In a direct encounter only first and second pronouns will do. But this point was not the one that transformed this fellow into a reformer with the aim of stopping, at any cost, the production of the advanced weapons of technological warfare. Buber goes on to say that the developing economic and political organizations tend to destroy the I-thou relation between persons in the society, in a snowballing growth that cannot be controlled even by the leaders *as persons*. Even they must become depersonalized agents in the efficient performance of their function. In short, organization gradually replaces community, leaving the organization man alone in the lonely crowd of people who then are referred to as he and she and it. The special significance of "you" and "I" wanes though they continue to be used for convenience, by people whose faces become abstract like Strelnikov's in Pasternak's *Dr. Zhivago*.

Now what bugged our hero was the way technological intelligence was augmenting this threat to human beings and being human. He was scared of atomic weapons. He was scared out of his wits, meaning that he resolved to take fanatic action. He became an organization man, as a leading member of The Organization Against Atomic Weapons. Enormous plants had been set up for producing these, supplying jobs for hundreds of thousands of people, some of whom were his best friends. He was himself a nuclear physicist and a professor of the subject in a good university. As a technical consultant he had learned some of the state secrets about national defense strategy.

The sonic boom that shattered the glass of his greenhouse was the last straw, symbolizing the final act of violation of all nature. He impulsively organized a march of BAN THE BOMB people in which the state secrets were writ large on placards. The Minister of Defense was forced to change quickly the pattern of production of atomic weapons and thousands of workers lost their jobs, some of whom had also kept gardens to preserve a sense of connection with nature. There followed a general withering of plants and human spirits. During the let-down, the Communists attacked and conquered. They had no qualms about any use of any weapons that served their purpose. Thus did the spiritual blight of collective farm plants and automated human beings take strangle hold, in the framework of an enforced materialistic philosophy. Our Anti-Bomb hero and the leading pacifists were offered influential positions in the new order, out of the enemy's gratitude for their contribution to the success of the new religion of technological control of THE PEOPLE, the liturgy of which consists in the psychological devices that reduce men to efficient instruments of THE CAUSE. Some of the pacifists accepted, in their conviction that loving living with anybody will show him the error of his ways. But our hero refused. Before he died in solitary confinement, he thought sadly about the mistake of supposing that technological development, which like any development is in organic relations with good things in life, can be thwarted by a single flamboyant move in the game of life-and-death. One must be careful about cutting out a cancer, lest the whole organism be destroyed. He remembered Auden who in his latter years was also saddened by the subtle violence that his earlier action of expatriation did to himself and to his country, instead of helping. Then they turned on him the new H-ray for etherealizing useless human instruments in ashless cremation, and the cell was left empty, clean, and shining for the next occupant.

10.

As I drove the straight long length of blacktop smooth as glass in the Arizona desert, I watched the thunder-head move across the highway ahead of me. It was two o'clock in the morning. I could tell the shape of the cumulus by the stars it blotted out in its passage. The lightning came in sheets of red light, revealing the convolutions of warm clouds and making the body of the storm transparent from within. The flashes were slow and enduring, as if resonant like echoes in the nebulous framework. I sensed this unity of light and sound and stepped on the accelerator to get closer. A few last drops splattered against the windshield as I got into the wake of the shower that had crossed my path ahead.

But now the stars were again above me as the dark source of noisy red light receded. I was alerted by the impression I had had of all these things going turbulently together, and listened with a new zest to the sound of the tires on the film of water on the road. The desert sand on both sides had absorbed it, and so was dark as Erebus. But the blacktop ahead had become a mirror reflecting the starlight above. I was alone on the empty highway. I turned off the headlights and drove by the starlight mirrored in a straight strip aimed at my destination far away. I suddenly felt that the music of the tires needed a supplement, so I stopped to take the air-filter for the oil off the motor, laying it on the floor of the car. I could then hear the car breathing with its iron lungs as it sucked in the clean air. It was as if the result were a little symphony that I was composing. I experienced this as interwoven into the larger composition of the night that began with the overture of the storm. The space and the time that I was travelling through was no longer just physical. Even my destination seemed now caught up and transfigured in the composition into my destiny. I saw a meteor flare ahead and disintegrate, its light echoing in the glassy surface of the route in front. I thought that it must have been too eager, too swift in its trip to where it could finally rest, and smiled as I brought my own speed down to fifty miles an hour. Besides, I could enjoy the passage on the thin straight river of starlight longer that way. Already it was losing its luster as I was getting to the edge of where the rain had fallen.

I had these thoughts not only in and with my mind. I was thinking with my blood and my whole body, which now included my car. I felt its response to my recognizing it as a part of myself. But my visual and auditory impressions were even more expansive. I was having these in the sky and in the dark face of the land. There was nothing subjective or inner about my impressions, in that situation. And I was grateful to technology for having given me my car. If it had been a horse and buggy, I would have worried about tiring the horse, and this would have disrupted my pervasive rapport with nature on that long trip. Then the thought occurred to me that technological know-how, so innocent in itself, was now being used to produce throw-away beer bottles, and I wondered when this would happen to cars. Maybe soon throw-away cars would be produced. You take a long trip in one, throw it away, and buy another one for the next trip. Good for the national economy. Why put up with the old thing for the two years that is now advertized as the standard duration for a respectable citizen? One year is better, and one trip better yet. The trend is toward throw-away cars. Naturally, this reflection dispelled my experience of community with nature and partly even with my own car. I found myself driving by a half-mile-long car dump beside the road. There lay the thrown away cars by the hundreds, I imagined.

Poor dears, I sense your mute appeal, from all the dismal car dumps in this vast land, to be cast into the fiery furnace and recast into shining new cars and re-animated as instruments in those little human pilgrimages that answer the call of that little god, the empty road. Some day I shall write the saga of motoring, to preserve the memory of you and put around you some of the glow of the affection that was denied you by your unfeeling drivers. . . .

The cancer is not technological intelligence. Nor is it any particular thing, in itself, that technology does or can produce. Not even the atom bomb. The cancer forms in another part of the human spirit as fear, or lust for domination, and the like. These are the sad effects of a sort of radio-active fall out of the uncontrolled exercise of technological know-how. Cutting these out without destroying the whole human complex is a problem not yet solved.

11.

What then is this technological intelligence, and the science that spawns it? Such general questions and the typical general answers are not very helpful. (Compare with, what is art? instead of, what is surrealism in art?) But some general considerations are worth making, nevertheless, in the vein of the descriptive metaphysics or phenomenology I've already sketched.

In the poetic thought and feeling of Rainer Maria Rilke there is a distinction between "thing" and "object" that can be brought out in the following way. Here I am expressing in these pages my love of things, in a familiar and intimate vein. Suppose I had said "my love of objects" instead, in that sentence. This would have given you a subtle jolt, not easy to analyze or explain. One speaks naturally of living things, not of living objects. Even when the thing, like your old coat, is not a living thing, it can, as a thing, be animated or come alive with meanings and values that make it hard to cast it off. But not as an object. You have, psychically speaking, to back off from the thing to become aware of it as an object. And in so doing, you become aware of yourself as a subject vis-à-vis the object. Moreover, the kind of subject you become is correlated with the kind of object the thing appears as, under the special sort of scrutiny that objectifies the thing while it subjectifies you. Please hang on here. The point I am making is crucial for a good philosophy of anything—a philosophy that does not begin with and get stuck with only one alternative for experience and thought, both of which have other real alternatives, from the ground up. I am making the point as clearly as I can. It has been featured in continental European philosophy and in literature everywhere. Kant, for example, had the same general idea. When you look at a thing in the special, controlled way called scientific observation, then it appears as a correspondingly special kind of object in scientific space and time, in causal relations to other such objects. Kant called these "phenomena," and the whole system of such objects he called "nature." Things appearing this way, as objects of observation, are not presented as they are simply "in themselves." These things-in-themselves are such that they may also appear as a moral order, a "kingdom of ends" whose members are free persons. But this way of looking at them is alternative to, and exclusive of, the scientific view of them. How to describe the relation between these two categorically different orders of appearances of things-in-themselves is for Kant quite a headache. In the end, he limits understanding to the phenomenal order of "observed" and scientifically construed objects, and leaves "rational faith" our only mode of access to the moral order of free moral agents. In his account of aesthetic experience, a sort of blend of these two orders occurs, suggesting their unity at the foundation of things.

But, unfortunately, Kant makes it look as if things as they simply are in themselves are completely beyond the pale of experience. According to him, there is no homely, non-special way of being with them, as elemental things among things. You've got to see them either as scientific objects or as free persons. And neither of these are things-in-themselves, simply. Each presupposes a fixed set of preconceptions, and these are the only angles of approach to things. Kant has nothing to say about a foundational experience, an earthy matrix, a milieu in which thing meets thing before such categorical distinctions are explicitly made. He overlooks the experience in which such distinctions are only implicit, as potentials for this or that special sort of experience and expression. Thus he also fails to notice the homely idiom of plain or familiar talk that has mushroomed out of the fertile soil of familiar experience, to serve as its mode of expression. (The new phenomenologists are presently doing what they can to rectify this mistake.) So, for Kant, there are persons to be loved—where love is good-will like the Christian *agape*—and natural objects to be used as instruments. To use persons and to love natural objects is a confusion and a mistake, according to Kant.

In one respect, Kant is right. If the thing in question is appearing as a physical object and being explicitly treated that way, it certainly does not, in that capacity, induce love of it. In that relationship, one is at the sort of psychic distance from it that abrogates the intimacy with it that is properly called love. One does not love things as just physical objects. Even Rilke would have agreed with this. But he would then have pointed out the more basic rapport with things as such (or *simpliciter* in the language of the learned), presupposed by the more sophisticated and exclusive modes of experience and expression. Things-in-themselves in this sense are not beyond the pale. In fact, they are so intimately present and so gravid with suggestions for this or that special kind of expression that the hardened specialist, committed to and educated within a special outlook and sensing the presence of such things, is tempted to say that they lie outside *all* experience and comprehension. This explains his mistake.

The moral for science and technology that comes out of this preamble is that they are not conversant "simply" or directly with things, but rather with things as objects of a special and exclusive sort. Let's call these physical objects, and let us say that this appearance is a "categorical aspect" of things. Or, we may say that under the category of the physical, a thing is seen as a physical object. Finally, let us call this mode of perception "observation" and the percipient subject of such experience an "empirical" or observing subject. Taking this sort of look at things, you are an "observer." Then the sort of account you will give of yourself as subject, in that rapport with things, will tend to be empirical. It will be primarily behavioral, also based on observation. At those points in such an account where the procedures of observational science seem not to apply, you will try to translate psychological reports into physicalistic equivalents, to satisfy the rule of confirmation by observation. The observers who, as specialists, forget or have never noticed that their mode of access to things involves, at base, a special way of looking at them, a categorical option, will be tempted to say that the observationally grounded account of things is the only "objective" one, since they will think that things simply are physical objects in the final analysis. They will suppose that the data of observational science are the only elements you will "see" so long as you are taking a good look at things. The rest is "subjective."

But the point that concerns me most here is one that even the trained observer will grant. Such a mode of perception purges feeling from the objective field of experience, while preserving a practical or operational relation to it. Moreover, it must be granted that it is *things* that are thus being experienced, explored, and manipulated. In short, science gives us a true view of the world. But, unlike some scientists, we must add: in *one* of its categorical aspects. That is, in one of its manifestations; the one in which observation, the scientific theories based on its data, and technological control of the phenomena are together the main business. Exploitation of things, living and non-living—including persons—will occur if this is mistaken as the only objective rapport with things, and the art of other categorically different approaches to things thus left uncultivated.

This affair of the categoreal aspects of a thing, and the change from one to another aspect which I shall call "aspection," is comparable to another (subordinate) kind of aspection that gets more notice, like that of the duck-rabbit picture. You may see this either as a duck, or by shifting gears so to speak, as a rabbit; never both these at once. Similarly, the picture, with perhaps a little more touching up to help, may be seen either as a physical or as an aesthetic object. If physical, the space of the picture-thing is determined by operational procedures—using units of measure, etc.—and in the end this structures the field even of observational *perception*, which is what is meant by its appearing as a physical object. You will notice that where the aspection is of this categoreal sort, the thing in question does not appear as something else, unlike the case of the picture appearing as a duck. But I must turn from these general considerations to some more impressions of technology and science. The detailing of the above soggy chunk of descriptive metaphysics will take place here and there in later reflections.

12.

Once there was a creature that went on all fours while it was young. Then it assumed an upright posture and maintained it, walking on its hind legs. Pretty soon the hind legs ceased to be hind because they were permanently beneath it, and its forelegs became arms with hands. It could then explore things by touch and manipulation. Thus what used to be forelegs became a tactual sense-organ with which it could feel out the nature of things in cooperation with its vision which, thanks to the upright posture, became the uppermost and dominant sense. The mouth that used to be brutally out in front receded and took its proper place beneath the eyes. It functioned there not only as an instrument of mastication but primarily as an organ of taste. Meanwhile, vision for this creature was becoming mainly an affair of recognition instead of just visual reaction to stimuli that excited appetite or fear. Along with these developments the brain behind and so close to the eyes became an organ of thought about things, but without losing its practical engagement with them through the arms that terminated, not in hoofs or claws, but in hands. Thus was the rugged connection with brute nature in and around it broken, and it needed another instrument of community with what was now not just the natural environment but a world. So it began to talk. In fact, this development did not come after the others. They all developed together, becoming more and more refined in a reciprocal collaboration and interpenetration. All this, especially the developing language, presupposed other such creatures, maturing together into human beings. Speaking the language became more and more the means not only of communication but of community and communion. It was these creatures' way of truly being together, who were all now in a kind of isolation from brute nature, as beings who had assumed the upright posture. They needed above all to talk, in speech forms that became their form of life, structuring the field even of their taste, touch and vision. Their language was their style of life, stylizing even most of their non-linguistic activities. But of course the language too was subject to influence and modification from these non-linguistic sources, so it too grew, ramified, and had a history. It made communion possible even with non-personal things. . . .

Irwin Straus has, in a fine bit of phenomenological description, made the above sort of point, about the upright posture, though I have made more than he did about the relation of standing and speaking. The more one ponders such a point, the more inclined he is to define a human being as the standing upright and speaking creature, and then to wonder which characteristic came first, in a question like that about the chicken and the egg. (A bird, by the way, is not upright in this sense. Its body tends toward the horizontal on its two legs. And see how its mouth protrudes forward beyond its eyes.) The most intriguing points related to this one are about the meanings that "up" and "down" have in the sort of space in which the upright being acts, feels and thinks—the space in which he lives and which is alive with his life. In this lived space or life-space, "up," "upright," "rectitude," "high," are expressive also of moral and religious values, suggesting aspiration, exaltation, and the like. And a downfall in such space is much more than the physical movement downward of a body. It can amount to degradation and defeat. Even the mountain climber senses these values of up and down, during the climb and the back-slidings. "Movement" in physical space is abstract compared with "action" in life-space. Similar remarks hold for "light" and "dark," in life-space. The important thing to notice here is that such meanings are elemental or original, *not* derived by a metaphorical twist performed on terms whose basic meaning was at first literal. The distinction between literal and metaphorical is a sophisticated one, emerging out of and presupposing the matrix of elemental significance that irradiates lived space or *Lebensraum*. Such an idea is at present getting important applications in what is called existential psychotherapy, aided and abetted by phenomenological considerations of the sort in Straus' essay. He is an M.D. at the Veterans Hospital in Lexington, Kentucky, collaborating with others in America and abroad in this snowballing enterprise of helping people who suffer from the abstractions of sophisticated intelligence that infest their vitality and humanity with psychosomatic complications.

13.

Let me now focus attention on the hand of the technologist. It is with this that he maintains what I called a practical relation to things. But it is a practical relation of a special sort. In the first place, the technologist's hand is not *simply* an instrument of getting him what he wants. It is an antenna of his scientific intelligence with which he feels out the nature of things, in the observational view of them. With his hands, he manipulates things to satisfy his theoretical demand for knowledge of them, though finding out what can then be done with them goes along with this and this is the strictly "technological" activity, as an expression of the power that Francis Bacon identified in too wholesale a fashion with scientific knowledge. They go together, but still the knowing-the-nature-of must be distinguished from the know-how. Technology as such is mainly concerned with the elaboration of the latter, "pure" science with the former. As an experimental scientist, a man uses his hands in the act of explorative thinking. He thinks with his hands. As a technologist, his hands are at work in the construction of artifacts, acting in a space that gets more and more purged of images and feeling as the work becomes mechanical and precise. Instead of seeing things animated with, say, aesthetic values, instead of manipulating things to make them more expressive of such values to be contemplated, he observes them in a network of metric patterns or schemata that serve as conceptual blue-prints for making instruments out of things. In such a process, things are more and more explicitly realized as physical objects in physical space. Perception of this sort, called observation, presents the data for this sort of conception, while the hand, at the work of technological construction, articulates or makes sense of both.

Now notice how the hand has less and less to do as the process becomes precise and powerful. In the early or cruder stages, the manual activity taxed the skill of the agent. Making the wooden plough, the wheel, blowing the bottle after coloring and fusing the glass. This was the period of masters and apprentices. In constructive work on this level, the whole man is active, though the activity is brought to a focus in the activity of the hand. Here there is not much sense of the separation from things simply as things. They have not yet been schematized into a world of explicitly physical objects, though this is the beginning of that. The spinning clay that takes shape as a pot under the molding influence of hands is a physical object in embryo. It is a work of art both in the technological and aesthetic sense of "art." The throw-away beer bottle that the machine spawns by the million is a full fledged physical object. You perceive and conceive it as such, usually. To maintain the elemental you-thing relation here, with its invitation for affectionate concern, takes an effort and even seems silly, sentimental. This is what I meant by the "psychic distance" from things that their realization as physical objects involves. This compresses the psyche more and more into a subjective or inner center, crowding it out of the environing world of things and thus leaving them denuded of the color and warmth that the expansive presence of the psyche among them confers.

As automation progresses, the work of the hand becomes less significant. It gets belittled. It is as if it too, like the psyche, gets crowded out of the theater of the important goings-on. It used to be engaged in what could properly be called human action. In the thoroughly automated situation, it itself functions like an automaton, making periodic little contributions to the whole automative process. What is worse, this automation reaches further back.

It automates the whole agent. It makes him look like a cog in the machine. I was going to say "feel" like a cog, but then I wondered what that could mean. Does a cog in a machine feel like one? Obviously, what people who use the expression have in mind is how out of place feeling of any sort is in a mechanized situation, which is what I was saying above.

A question may have come up as to why and how *images* must be extruded from the field of scientifically controlled observation. That feelings must be so excluded may seem clearer. What about the scientific imagination? Years ago I dealt with this question in an essay that has been anthologized twice. Since it shows rather nicely what I used to think about this, I present it again in the following section. I say "used to," because I now realize that my earlier notion of the imagination was too strait. Let me say some more things about it, including its function in science, at a later time.

14[a].

Pictorial Meaning and Picture Thinking

Professor Charles W. Morris, in his essay "Empiricism, Religion, and Democracy," writes:

> Imagine a community of men living on a cell in the blood stream of one of us, but so small that we have no evidence, direct or indirect, of their existence. Imagine further that they themselves are provided with scientific instruments of the type we use, and possess a method of science and a body of scientific knowledge comparable to ours. One of the bolder of these thinkers proposes that the universe they inhabit is a Great Man. Is this hypothesis admissible on scientific grounds or is it to be laughed down by the Minute Empiricists on the ground that it is "metaphysical"? We Macroscopic Empiricists would at least seem to have to favor the hypothesis! But then why at our own level cannot a similar hypothesis be raised: namely, that

we are parts of a Great Man, the whole of our known universe being perhaps but a portion of the Great Blood Stream? ... The liberal empiricist I have championed would side with the Minute Empiricists in asserting that the hypothesis is empirically meaningful since the properties ascribed to the Great Man would be properties drawn from objects that had been observed; he would merely say that in terms of evidence available to them this hypothesis was too poorly confirmed to have a place in their system of scientific knowledge.

I have quoted Morris at length, because the excerpt highlights the point to the examination of which this essay is given, namely, the concept of "empirically significant possibilities" and a way of treating it which persists despite recent refinements in the general theory of meaning—a way I take to be inadequate. If as competent a specialist in the theory of signs as Morris (and C. I. Lewis) can go wrong on this count, it is little wonder that the mistake is such a common one among those who have given the matter less systematic attention. The matter concerns a kind of meaning, or a way of using language, that has not been isolated with sufficient rigor from other kinds, the result being a tendency to accommodate it under the general category of cognitive sense, to the detriment of both kinds, as we shall see. The ill-advised mixture converts both into renegades that frequently lead inquiry and discussion into an impasse.

Another illustration—and yet others later—will help us to detect, isolate, and tag the new kind of sense.

Suppose someone—whom we shall call Typical Tom—says there is a little blue devil in his watch. We open it and find nothing but the usual mechanism. Tom says the little devil disappears into thin air the moment the watch is opened. We then weigh the watch, when it is open and again when it is closed, noticing no difference in weight. Tom says the little blue imp, like any genuine spirit, is an immaterial and therefore imponderable substance. Then we observe that the watch keeps time accurately, which would be unlikely with a blue devil inside, getting its tail and legs caught in the gears and hairspring. Well, we can guess what Tom says to that. And so on.

To such a position as Tom's there are four usual reactions. The first, and least cautious, is the assertion that Tom's blue-devil utterance is patently false. But a plainly false expression is, by definition, one that can be disproved; and there is *no* way to disprove, there is *no* evidence against, what Tom says. The second reaction to it is the more cautious objection that he's talking nonsense—making "pure nonsense," which explains our inability to prove the falsity of his utterance. But even little children could clearly understand—and be delighted by—Tom's remark, and would clamor for its expansion into a story about the little blue devil. So evidently Tom has made himself intelligible in some sense. A third reaction might be the suggestion that Tom's utterance is indeed significant but only with motivational or emotive meaning. (In Morris' own terminology, one night say Tom's expression contains "motivators" or "expressors," but no "referors.") But Tom correctly points out that, for him, the blue-devil utterance did not express a mood or feeling, neither was it aimed at getting somebody to do something.

Suppose now we ask Tom how he *knows* that a little blue devil haunts his watch, pointing out that one can *imagine* the presence or absence of anything in it. He then concedes that his original statement, "It is *true* that there is a little blue devil in my watch," is too strong, and weakens it to read, "It is just *possible* that there is . . . etc."

This, I take it, is the position that Morris would assume, adding of course, as he did in the Blood Stream case, that the blue-devil hypothesis is "too poorly confirmed to have a place in the system of scientific knowledge." Moreover, this conclusion seems in general so harmless from any point of view—that of the scientist, artist, speculative cosmologist, theologian, moralist—that it is the one most commonly arrived at. It has, in addition, the air of being "liberal," inasmuch as it seems to give the speculative imagination the important place it apparently has even in the field of scientific inquiry. Such difficulties have appeared only after analysis of meaning has been pressed beyond the province of specific interests. For general methodology, pressing the analysis, further is crucial and shows the way out of verbal predicaments even on the level of common discourse—predicaments that are simply battered down out of the way (instead of being solved) by disputants who don't understand them. So let us try to formulate—here necessarily in a rough and popular way—certain distinctions.

The main point we are going to make is that Tom's utterance, "It is possible that there is a little blue devil in the watch," is comparable to the expression, "It is possible that please go away." As the expression "please go away" does not make cognitive sense—it is neither true nor false—but motivational, so the expression "There is a little blue devil in the watch" does not make cognitive sense but (what we shall call) *pictorial* sense. Our task now is to so define pictorial meaning as to disengage it from the cognitive with which it is so readily confused, and to explain why the confusion is so prevalent. With this task we now come to grips.

Discourse frequently takes a turn that makes argument concerning its subject-matter irrelevant. But this happens in at least two quite different ways. That there is a grain of sand in the watch is arguable. That there is a neutrino in the watch is also appropriately argued. But people would naturally refuse even to argue the proposition that the mechanism of the watch consists of nothing but thirteen hydrogen atoms, because the proposition is too plainly false. They would be annoyed with anyone who would continue elaborating such a position. This is *one* way in which argument becomes irrelevant. But suppose it were said that the watch is the cosy habitat of an army of a million little archers, each armored in mother-of-pearl and bearing a bow made of a splinter of diamond, all too small ever to be observed; and when the watch is closed it is filled with a soft, iridescent radiance — the light of their world; each tick of the watch marks off a day in their lives and an hour a life-span; they are unerring marksmen, capable in that twilight of knocking the spinning electrons out of their orbits with their golden arrows . . . .

Now in this case also we would find argument irrelevant, but is it because the utterance is too plainly false, or, in Morris' words, "too poorly confirmed?" This would be an inadequate estimate, since there is *no* possible evidence against the utterance, and it may be "poorly confirmed" in the sense that "please go away" is poorly confirmed, neither expression being the sort with respect to which the demand for evidence is relevant.

But the important point is that in this case of the archer, far from being annoyed at the elaboration of such a position, we *want more*. It is as if the sense that is now being made lies in a different dimension of meaning, or differs in kind, from that of the expressions concerning the grain of sand, the neutrino, and the thirteen hydrogen atoms. We have shifted gears into a different form of discourse, which in its own way may be highly intelligible and even important (if charged also with emotive and motivational significance) without formulating an empirically significant "possibility" awaiting confirmation. We shall call such meaning "pictorial" and we call its formulation "picture thinking."

One is tempted to object that all four of the above expressions formulate empirically significant possibilities, the only difference being that the archer possibility is so much more picturesque than the others (sand, neutrino, etc.) that we naturally incline to contemplate and enjoy it for its own sake, thus ignoring the question—which nevertheless remains relevant—of its truth or falsity. In short, it formulates an empirically significant possibility.

The answer to this hinges mostly on a terminological issue: people who say that a sentence formulates an "empirically possible" state of affairs usually mean that it is true or false and that some day it *might* be confirmed or infirmed [discomfirmed]. (This, I take it, is what Morris means, it is true or false that there are little men on a blood cell in one of us, and if we had fine enough instruments and if there *are* little men on blood cells we would detect their existence, etc.) But the archer-situation has been so couched (or could be) as not only to make proof or disproof impossible but to make the demand for either irrelevant, while retaining a very clear-cut intelligibility of the pictorial sort. We conclude, therefore, that language can be used with the primary intention of expressing or evoking pictures (imagery), and in a way that differs from the sign usage that formulates empirically significant possibilities.

So far, our illustrations have involved cases where the pictorial intent is so salient as to be fairly readily distinguished from the cognitive or empirical. We don't ordinarily argue the blue devil or archer utterances because we "get," by a kind of linguistic instinct or habitual propriety, what the speaker primarily means by them. His primary intention is obvious, namely, to tease and entertain us (and himself) with pictures that, as verbally treated by him, have nothing to do even with *possibilities* for matters of fact.

14[b].

But pictorial sense can be made of practically anything, and *this may be the only kind of sense that is being made even where the aim is to make statements about matters of fact.* It is in such cases that disputants reach an impasse, which blocks them until a distinction is made between the pictorial and the cognitive content of the expression in question. Instances of such predicaments are common. Let us examine some.

We are looking at a scarf and "observe" that, in a certain light, it is "red." Typical Tom says that maybe it isn't "really" red. We call in others to take a look, or ourselves look more closely, or even make measurements of wave-frequency, etc., getting a confirmation of our judgment. But Tom says that what he means by "red" is a visual sensation in each one of our minds and, for all we will ever know, no two of these sensations are alike. Yours may actually be blue while mine is green, though both of us have been taught to say "red" when we are aware of these color patches as data in our minds.

Now it would be a mistake to say wholesale that Tom is talking nonsense. He evidently "means" something by these remarks and, moreover, most of us "get" something at the receiver's end of the communication. What is evoked in most of us by the utterance is a set of pictures, such as two non-overlapping, translucent spheres ("minds") inside one of which we imagine a tiny blue patch and a green patch in the other, as effects of streams of light radiation reaching the spheres from a common external source. Then, if we imagine each of these spheres as hovering near the head of a human organism which says "red" when the color patch appears in its sphere, the picture is complete, and we have understood what Tom said. But his primary intention in this case is to say something that might be true of matters of fact, something that is "just possible." Has he succeeded in this? The fact that he has not said anything demonstrably *false* must not, it should be remembered, be taken by itself as a sign of his having formulated an empirically significant possibility, for reasons noted above. An examination of what Tom put across by his utterance shows that he has made himself intelligible in the dimension of pictorial meaning. But that he has made sense of any other than the blue devil kind is doubtful. And if, objecting to the picturesque turn we have given his expression, he attempts a "literal" interpretation, he will, in this quest for its empirical (cognitive) meaning, find himself looking in a dark room for a black cat that isn't there. ("Attempting a literal interpretation" means, of course, trying to get the expression coordinated with some matters of fact that serve as evidence for or against it; but it has been so worded as to preclude this possibility.) It is the function of the philosophical analyst to show Tom that, with respect to cognitive significance, he has failed to understand himself, since, in that dimension of meaning, he has either said nothing, or something so ill-defined as to be unintelligible without preliminary (and perhaps strange) linguistic conventions. But this, of course, does not militate against the intelligibility of the expression in its dimension of pictorial significance.

Current discussion of the dimensions of space provide us with another illustration of how one may make pictorial sense only, while intending to say something true about matters of fact. People say they "observe" up to three dimensions, but can't even "imagine" a fourth. Typical Tom, associating the "possible" with the "imaginable," concludes from this that the hyperspace theorists don't know what they are talking about. (Even Poincare suggests that someday we may be able, after strenuous exercise, to "imagine a fourth dimension," whereupon non-Euclidean geometry will possibly become more "convenient" than the Euclidean.) But this is to make the mistake of supposing that when we say,

"Space has *n* dimensions," the pictures evoked by the expression define its cognitive meaning. Strictly speaking, the cognitive sense even of the expression, "Space has three dimensions," is left untouched by what one can or can't imagine: what this expression means empirically, through operational definitions, is as "unimaginable" as the one about four or more dimensions. Or, putting it yet another way, the sense in which three dimensions *can* be "observed" or "imagined" is precisely the sense in which the fourth dimension can be observed or imagined; in both cases, something is to be observed that proves or disproves the propositions about space, and in the same general way.

The writings of Jeans and Eddington are a fertile source of illustrations of our point about pictorial meaning. "There is a mysterious world outside us to which our minds can never penetrate"; an "inscrutable absolute behind appearances," etc. The analysis of such expressions in the light of the distinction made above is obvious, so we shall not here given them special attention. Our moral is that one should be on guard against the little blue devil, since he can assume many shapes as, if undetected, be-devil discourse in a very tantalizing way.

But special attention should be given something that so far we have dealt with only implicitly. From an inspection of linguistic properties or grammatical form alone, one cannot safely tell what the primary intention of the speaker is. Typical Tom, upon looking into the watch or into the Mexican jumping bean and seeing no little blue devils might well have admitted at once that he was wrong. This would show that he not only intended to make empirical (factual) sense, but actually did. He was construing "blue devil" in a factually significant way. On the other hand, blue-devil sense (pictorial) might readily be made even of the expression about the grain of sand in the watch. Tom might teasingly say, upon not observing one inside, that there is one there anyway, only of a peculiar invisible sort, etc. This is what we meant by saying that practically anything can be construed pictorially, in a way that does not limit or define even a *possible* state of affairs for matters of fact. Thus, pictorial sense can be made even of objects in the field of sense-perception, and the artist makes a profession of this. Morris' mistake was the initial one of supposing that his little-men hypothesis about an object of perception, namely a blood cell, formulated an empirically significant possibility. From this mistaken assumption he argued the cognitive significance of the hypothesis of our being caught in a Cosmic Blood Stream or parts of a Great Man.

Traditionally, "theory" and "cognition" (knowledge) have meant some involving contemplation and spectacle—"vision," with emphasis on picture-thinking and pictorial meaning. This essay would be properly doom to the limbo of all dogmatisms if its thesis were either that the words "theory" and "knowledge" and "cognitive significance" *cannot* mean these things, or that pictorially significant sign-usage is unimportant. Its thesis is, rather, that since even the traditional theorists tended to argue what they called "theories," and since pictorial meaning is intrinsically non-arguable, as we have seen after isolating it from another sort that is arguable, we had better let "theory" and "cognitive meaning" involve this latter kind of sense and preclude the former. There is nothing anti-liberal in such a proposal. Indeed, it is aimed at liberating both the intellect and the imagination each for its special task. It explains, moreover, the sense one has of "understanding" an expression before it is in any way cognitively coordinated with matters of fact—such understanding being a grasp of pictorial significance.

The popular (and half true) notion that even the task of the scientist is implemented by a lively imagination here calls for comment. It has been noted that we have not, existentially speaking, drawn a line between a "field (or realm) of imagination" and a "field of sense-perception," confining the scientist to the latter. In fact, we flout the distinction by saying that, given *any* item, whether perceived or imagined, then either pictorial or cognitive sense can be made of it, according to the way in which it is construed and articulated. That is why much of the experimental work of the great scientist can be (and usually is) of the arm-chair variety. Not that he is, in such moments, doing what the poet or artist does, but rather that he is articulating imagined states of affairs in empirically (factually) significant propositions. This is the crucial difference. The notion that the great theorist is necessarily half-poet is mistaken and misleading. Of course, he may also be a poet, but not with respect to theoretic acumen. Much of the published work of theorists such as Eddington, Montague, Santayana, and others, great though it is as a provocative for thought and imagination, is marred by the failure to distinguish theorizing from picture thinking.

15.

On second thought, there is more to be said about the impression of a man's becoming a cog in a machine in a thoroughly automated situation. First, a distinction must be made between the technologists in the vanguard of new discoveries, constructions, and uses of instruments. These people have no cog-like feelings at all. It is a wrapt and absorbing adventure. For example, the technologists who produce the rocket that boosts the capsule into orbit around the earth. They are creators, and excited about it. So is the secondary sort of technologist who is taught to occupy the capsule, even if he does not need to use the manual controls during the flight because the automatic controls do all the work perfectly. There is room for feeling in such situations, even for an earthy prayer by the orbiting technologist aimed at heaven during the flight, expressing the wonder of things and gratitude for the achievement. All this is a stupendous action that has, in that reference-frame, the quality of still being human. The automation that gets a man down or reduces him to a cog in a machine is the sort that replaces a human action with a mechanical. The automated carving knife, for example. With such an instrument, carving loses the name of action. It becomes an oscillatory movement of a physical object on a physical object—the roast—in physical space. The function of the carver's hand is belittled into an insignificant directional one. The dynamics of the art of carving is reduced to the statics of mere cutting. Where there is no action of manual slicing there is no carving. This sort of replacement of human actions by mechanical processes is going on in a multitude of various ways. The latest sewing machines, for example. You can "embroider" with them, without learning how to embroider. Notice that those two uses of the term are not at all equivalent. Only the latter refers to a human action. The art of embroidering is going down the drain. This is not a protest against the use of the sewing machine to do the enormous quantities of common sewing that needs to be done. It protests, rather against loading them with devices that do what it were better for the unaided human hand to do, in a disciplined expression of human affection for the clothes that have it in them to become parts of us. Things that are hand stitched are still advertised as something special, but this premium put on manual needle-work has diminished considerably, in ray time. Circumstances are forcing it to look increasingly plaintive and sentimental. Maybe they are making little, expressive human actions such as these impossible, by eliminating the option in their favor. We are having less and less choice in the matter, perhaps. This is what I meant by technological determinism. And this is what I am worrying about.

Finally, the automation that hurts is the sort that mechanizes the operation of the common laborer in factory and plant, by withering his hand and then the whole agent. Such people are not only servants of technology as anyone is in its ambit. We have seen that the servants in the vanguard, or up front in the area of creative advance, can still be human. These are servants only in the sense of being creatures in the sphere of influence — determined by the thrust — of a growing technology. But the plant or factory worker is servant in the sense of slave. He is a thoroughly automated part of the machine, one of its cogs; not its designer. He is a mere means, with the end completely out of sight. John Dewey also worried about any theater of operations in which there is this stark separation of means from ends. Human action is impossible in such a space. One reason that his philosophy of human nature has fallen from public grace is that the tide of technological development is against it or, better, that the philosophy is against the tide.

Tides always win. The commonly professed reason for his philosophy's failure is that it bucked the tide of theology. This too was a reason, but a minor one.

I confess that the vein I have been talking in about the unfortunate effects of technology on humanity makes me feel a bit silly. The charge that it is sentimental would have considerable justification. But some such warning has to be issued and I shall continue doing my part in the job. What complicates the task for me is that I feel counter-tendencies to praise, even to love, the gadgets that technology is showering on us in the twentieth century. Still, there is something gravely wrong and some protest, couched one way or another, must be made.

Coming out of what I have rightly or wrongly said, however, is an issue about which important things are being asserted in the new philosophy of language and which I can be more confident about. The tremendous expansion of the technological consciousness and the field of its operations has tempted many people to suppose, not only that in principle a machine can do anything that a human being can, but that a human being is itself a complex and delicate machine beyond our power *at present* to produce. (I advisedly say "itself" not "himself.") The notion has a different complexion from that of old style materialism because it emphasizes not just the stuff out of which human beings are made—matter—but the functions. This is given a new twist by logical and linguistic considerations of statements of what various sorts of things do or are capable of doing. The concept of human action is thereby put on the spot. For example, we speak of washing machines, talking machines, writing machines (typewriters), adding machines, computers. In fact, we have such machines, the biggest and best of which, the IBM's, can even give us translations of languages. But we do not speak of, say, thinking machines. Do we have them anyway? Are *we* such?

The new linguistic or conceptual style of treatment of this whole issue is nicely pinpointed in the recent cartoon that showed a technologist boasting about the big IBM to a visiting lady. The caption has the lady saying: "So it can think, but can it change its mind?" There is a subtle *double entendre* in this. On the one hand, the visitor seems to admit that the machine can think while, on the other, casting some suspicion even on this by suggesting that it can't change its mind. Anyway, it is this notion of certain concepts going together or forming conceptual families that present-day philosophers of language are stressing, due to Wittgenstein. Sever any one of such concepts from this vital connection, and it collapses into nonsense. That is to say, if you significantly say of something that it can think, it must be significant—though perhaps false in a given case—to say of it also that it can change its mind, since these concepts go together by an informal logic of the expressions. If you are not prepared to say that the machine can change its mind—which is different from being able to correct for "errors" in calculation—you should be unprepared to say that it can think.

Such families of expressions can be quite large, with borderline or doubtful membership near the boundaries. For example, is the machine elated by successfully accomplishing an elaborate and thoughtful investigation? Is it disappointed by breakdowns? Does it hope and plan to do better? If these questions applied to the machine puzzle us, should we be puzzled also by the question, does or can it think? My impression is that we should, and this is in accord with the new linguistic and phenomenological treatment of the subject. But, can it make mistakes or errors? Here we have one of those borderline cases, since "mistake" has some uses that loosen its connection with strictly human actions such as thinking. Thus, whether or not it can go wrong is more independent of the question of its ability to think.

Notice the spirit of this sort of treatment of the issue. We are not intending primarily to make judgments about the ultimate nature of anything. Rather, we are looking at terms and concepts in clusters, and wondering about the relationships to one another that are conditions of their significance. The upshot for "thinking" and "machine" is that they curdle or don't make sense when juxtaposed in phrases with the grammatical form either of questions or declarative sentences.

But what now of, say, the washing machine and the typewriter? Can a machine wash? Can a machine write? The first impulse here is to answer, of course. But accompanying this is as strong an impulse to add that what this means is that a *human being* can wash with a machine and write with one. This is in contrast with his inability to think or will or feel with a machine. (*Some* forms of thinking, such as calculating, he *can* do with a machine; so we have calculating machines.) The curious thing is, however, that even of a washing or typing machine one might whimsically ask, when did it decide to do the washing or the writing it is now doing? ("Deciding to do" goes along with "human action"; they are members of a family of concepts.) This would be to drive home the significance of these operations as human actions. And the point is that, for such cases, the questions can significantly be translated into: when did *you* decide to write or wash with the machine? suggesting that the action retains its quality of being human as long as the mechanical instrument serves the purpose so well— often better than would the unaided hand. In short, one can press the return-to-raw-nature note too much in the plan to keep our selves human. Take, for example, a "manuscript." Must we insist that, strictly, nothing is a manuscript that is not written with the hand's finger dipped in ink? Doesn't using even just a stylus or pen denature handwriting into an (elementary) mechanical process? And more so if it is a typewriter? (Here we do sometimes call the result a "typescript.") But surely the answer to this is that, in general, any instrument or mechanical device that can become a part of oneself in action, by serving the purpose so well, is *not* a dehumanizing factor. On the contrary, it broadens the scope of human action. We need, as human beings, to sew and write. We need machines to help us do these. But we also need to embroider, carve, and fight, upon occasion. So we must be on guard against the technological devices the use of which requires us to put the words for these activities in scare-quotes. A human being can't really carve or embroider with a machine that takes the essential artfulness out of the action. For these, needles and unelectrified knives are necessary. They become parts of you in the process. Similarly for fighting. We need sometimes really to fight, and this is possible only with weapons that can be incorporated in the action. No scare-quotes around the term. With atom bombs thrown in, the very notions of "weapon," "soldier," "going to war" become senseless. Instead of weapons that are parts of the fighter, he functions himself as a part or cog in the machine of destructive conflict. Notice that the main objection to using atom bombs is here that one cannot really fight with them, something he tragically needs to do on occasion. This is quite distinct from the objection more commonly made, that atomic warfare destroys life so indiscriminately. Such an objection makes it look as if thermonuclear destruction is a human action and immoral because of its terrible consequences. This way of putting it twists a point that, when straightened out, is a good one. But my point is that when we get caught up in the maelstrom of thermonuclear energies released by pressing a button, we become parts of a total automated process and are therefore not fighting for anything, since the behavior of the elements of such a system—including us—is not human action. In short, it is a-moral. Thus, even the notion of tragedy becomes senseless in such a situation. Extermination, yes, but not tragic. This situation is indeed a terrible trap for *human* beings to get caught in. What is most terrible about it is not that it is so immoral but that it is so thoroughly dehumanized. There is a reduction to a condition in which nothing that goes on can count either as moral or immoral. Nobility and tragedy have disappeared from the picture. Perhaps you can see now that my objection to atomic conflict is more subtle than the common one about its wickedness. It is like the objection to the notion that a machine can paint a picture, or be blamed for doing a bad one.

Speaking of subtleties, many subtle distinctions between kinds of human actions have been overlooked in this meditation. Some of these seem to "mean to be" artful, if I may put it that way. Embroidering, for example. We must be careful about technological "aids" in such connections. Others, like shaving or common sewing, are such that an "efficient" performance is the main thing. Such do not lose the name of human action by the employment of mechanical instruments as automated as you like, or as serve the purpose. But enough of all this for now. My aim has been to tell you something about the new way of looking at philosophical pronouncements such as those about what machines can do, and people being machines, and the like. What has come to light is a new criterion of making sense, in the form of the notion of families of terms that are related by an informal logic. The test for a term's making sense is its continuing to be useful—not puzzling when joined to other members of the family. "A man is a machine." Well, a man thinks, and he *decides* to think something through. Can this be said of a machine? "Deciding" and "being a machine" belong to different families of concepts, so cannot be significantly applied to the same thing. Notice that all such assertions of what "cannot" be the case are in effect not about a certain impotence of *things*, rather about what can significantly be *said* about them. And the upshot, for men and machines, is that (1) a man can do all sorts of things with technological devices, though sometimes the use of these prevents him from performing the sort of human action he needs to do and thinks he is doing with the machine; he may just think he is embroidering while he is actually only mechanically decorating, or only pushing a button and killing while supposing himself to be fighting; (2) it is a complete mistake, logically speaking, to suppose that the machine *per se* ever performs any of these human actions, this implying that the man himself, the final agent, cannot significantly be supposed to be a machine; (3) yet it is true that the automation going on in the field of human behavior is tending to pre-empt it, attenuating it into activities that are less expressive of the individual agent as a human being who thus, in *this* sense, is getting mechanized in the process.

In a fairly recent essay I exhibited this new fashion in philosophy of language. Also, it gets me beyond the position I took about pictorial meaning and picture thinking. It shows how images that we have as we speak may influence us into violating the above principle of meaningfulness. So I spread it before you in the following section. In it, I have again made some mistakes, especially in the account of technological invention as involving prehension or "seeing as." This stretches the notion of that mode of perception too far. In subsequent reflections, I shall rectify this error, showing that scientific imagination is *not* a form of *seeing* something as something.

[There is no Section 16 in Aldrich's typescript.]

17.

Image Mongering and Image Management

Wittgenstein asked if one could imagine a stone's "having consciousness," and said much to the effect that, even if one can, such "image-mongering" does not have the sort of significance that some philosophers suppose it to have in relation to questions of what is possible or meaningful. This notion image-mongering, together with that of its correlate which I call image-management, is what I propose to explore here. The former will be shown to be an ineffectual spawning of images with no significance even for what is "possibly" the case, while the latter puts images to constructive use in various ways.

Let us examine first a series of questions in an order of increasing perplexity: could a Japanese ten-year-old child talk English, could a human imbecile talk English, could a parrot talk English? Could a lion, could a human-shaped machine, could a cannon ball, could a stone talk English?

Such "could" questions are sometimes interpreted as answerable in the affirmative, provided only that the corresponding affirmative statements involve no contradictions. And this, of course, would be to construe "could x be P" as "is x's being P logically possible?" All the above questions are answered affirmatively in this light. So are the questions: could the relation of blue to high C on the keyboard talk English, could the $\sqrt{-1}$ talk English? Yes, is the answer, under this criterion and this interpretation.

But obviously this treatment is not sufficient as an account of the increasing strangeness of our series of questions. In short, it is not at all a theory of *meaning* of words and phrases in relation to the world. To take care of this deficiency, an observational verification-in-principle criterion of meaning is sometimes proposed; and then the question becomes, what *could* be verified thus? To save this "could" from reverting back to the purely logical, empty concept of possibility sketched above, imagination is brought in to decide what is "factually" possible. Whatever you can imagine to be the case "could" be so in fact, people say, including Hume. This, it is claimed, will show what is wrong with some of the questions in our series, with respect to meaning.

Well, let us unleash our imaginations; let us turn them loose on our questions of what *could* be the case. The Japanese ten-year-old is readily disposed of. Of course he could speak English. We can imagine it, *never mind the circumstances.* Even without his receiving any instruction, we can *imagine* him mouthing, all at once, a fine passage from Shakespeare. As for the imbecile, the same holds. Just put him in the field of the auditory imagination, and we can hear him saying anything you please. With our imagination on this sort of spree, the parrot and the lion get exactly the same treatment as the Japanese and the imbecile. We have a moment's hesitation over the machine, but since it is shaped like a man and has an aperture in roughly the right place in the front of its head, we can imagine that "mouth" grinding out, or "talking," English. The cannon ball and the stone present a special difficulty. What are we to imagine them as talking with? One way out is to imagine them as developing a sort of crimp on one side, softening that up bit, and then talking with it, like the moon with the help of the man-on-the-moon. But if this is cheating at this game — *can* one cheat at this game of the imagination on the loose? — we can imagine these round, hard, smooth things without mouths bouncing on the floor to the pattern of the Morse code, and thus saying or tapping out something to us that could be put into the King's English. Thus they could talk without mouths. But why be so scrupulous all at once? We could just imagine a flow of English coming from their surface, like an echo from a cliff. This can be *imagined* to be their way of talking. We could even get used to it, and get over the idea that it is a kind of echoing.

And *this* image of a thin stream of English words reaching us from never-mind-what kind of source can be conjured up even in the cases of the $\sqrt{-1}$ and the relation between blue and high C, though here a picturable image of the source would (perhaps) be lacking, and this may be cooked up into a reason for excluding such cases as nonsensical.

But, if the above account of imagining what could be the case is accepted, and this is taken as the criterion of meaning, then all the above cases down to and including the stone's are not only logically possible, but are significant of what could happen in the world, this evening. (Those of us who are really ingenious at this game might manage to include even the high C / blue relation and the $\sqrt{-1}$ in this picture.) In short, we would say on this basis that we *understand* the expressions right down to—and maybe including—the last two cases, and add that, as things are at present, of course it is "probably false" that lions, etc., do talk English. We must say "probably," because right now in Africa a lion may be mystifying his lioness-love in the silent moonlight by softly growling to her a line from Keats: "Thou still unravished bride of quietness…" We can imagine it, ergo, it makes sense, and could be the case—though in fact not likely.

Proceeding this way, we are left with the feeling that our inquiry into meaning and possibility is again slipping or skidding on a frictionless surface (Wittgenstein), much as at first, when we were making the purely logical point about contradiction. The smooth glossing over is still here. We are not yet breaking ground in support of the answer to our *real* question about what "could" be the case. Our imagination was not working at anything or in gear with anything. It was idling; it was not even playing. When it plays, it *constructs* something, namely, a story, a tale that people understand and love, without the perplexity generated by our line of talk in the above examples. I call this bewildering thing, not "imagining" anything, but simply "imaging." Wittgenstein called it image-mongering.

We sensed that something was beginning to slip when we passed from the Japanese child's case and the imbecile's where our question had a use, on to the parrot's and the others, giving *all* the same treatment as if there were no logical differences. We feel that the first two are "real" questions, the others not. And all this is accounted for by noticing that what was lacking is a concern for the meaning of the terms. And the imaging or image-mongering did not disclose or supply a meaning. It left the question wide open. It skidded right over its smooth surface, as if the terms "imbecile," "robot," "talking," etc., are intuitively understood *in the abstract* and their significant combinations to be decided by sheer fancy or imaging, thus overlooking the crucial difference between conceiving and imaging—*imaging*, I say; not imagining.

We must also notice that the question of logical possibility itself cannot be decided until the question of what *concepts* are involved is answered; that is, what the terms and phrases mean. Only then can we significantly say what could be the case. Our image-mongering did not come to grips with this question. Thus, neither pure formal logic nor sheer imaging, nor these combined, will tell us whether, say, a lion could talk. The answer will depend on what is meant by "lion" and "talk." Wittgenstein drives this point home by saying that even if a lion could talk, we would not understand him. A characteristically teasing remark. This is a challenging way of saying that were we confronted with a case of a lion seeming to talk a language, we would put one or both of these terms in scare-quotes — it is mouthing the language, it is not a lion, we are dreaming etc., — or this would be an occasion for the collapse of one or both concepts and, *pro tem.*, we would be unable to make sense of it; we would not know what to say, "lion" and "talk" meaning what they do in our language. But the main point is that *this would not simply be an empirical discovery that lions can talk*. This *sort* of point is the nerve of Kant's criticism of Hume's imagistic treatment of meaning and possibility questions. The issue is a logical one about the relation of concepts, not a psychological question as to who can produce what image-clusters, or simply have certain images.

Some of us are doubtless remembering at this juncture the standard way to make the distinction between the two senses of "could." In one sense, there is a reference to "circumstances." Thus one says that something could or could not be the case in such-and-such circumstances. This, it is commonly said, distinguishes factual or "real" possibility from the purely logical sort. For example, if the Japanese child were normal and had had proper instruction in English—with other such qualifications—then he "could" talk it, and would. These circumstances would include the assumption of certain inductively grounded laws of nature, etc. But, in the other sense of "could," the logical one, we abstract from all such circumstances, simply relating the two concepts "Japanese child" and "talking English," intuitively grasped in the empty logical-space of pure possibility that is left when the whole world drops beneath consideration or notice. Then the answer to the "could" question is an *a priori* affirmative. In this vacuum, the concepts are compatible; and that is all we need to know to answer the question thus interpreted. The machine-talking-English case is treated by some in exactly the same way. In the circumstances, it "could" not talk; but, logically speaking, it could. Saying so involves no contradiction. And what is logically possible *may* be realized in fact. We can imagine it. Thus imagination is taken as converting the logically possible into a thin sort of factual possibility.

What is wrong with this last assertion is that it treats "talking," "imbecile," etc., as if they were like logical or form words with a constant and self-contained meaning, independent of the circumstances of their use. The point, as against this procedure, is that these concepts become indeterminate in such isolation. They collapse into sheer images which are spawned by the absence of the circumstantial controls that are necessary to conceiving anything, as distinct from image-mongering. They cease to become thing-words and become verbal occasions for fancying *ad lib*, with no implications for what could be the case *for any matters of fact*. The latter is what is generally overlooked. It is still supposed that, though the logical "could" is now in point, it indicates a quite general fact about the world *via what is being simply imaged*. This is supposed to show that any damn thing you like is abstractly possible here and now even in these circumstances, as if the sheer imaging or image-mongering significantly determined such possibilities. The trouble is that the people who talk this way about the abstract "could" think that they are asserting something more than that the expressions involve no contradictions. When they go on to the imaging, they have the world in mind and think they are saying something meaningful and true about what could be the case *in it*. They are prepared to tell me that right now I *could* be a robot with no mind of my own, only mouthing English at them. Of course, people who say this will smile reassuringly, adding that all this is highly improbable. Their concluding remark, however, is usually "but it *could* be the case, right here and now, in the circumstances." It stretches the imagination to discover this fact, they admit, but is not that a wholesome exercise? Philosophy *begins* in wonder. Why should it not *end* in downright amazement?

The answer to this line of talk is suggested by examining another case that also required a great stretch of the imagination, but is plainly of a different *logical* stripe. Take the case, not of the talking machine, but of the flying machine. Back in Leonardo da Vinci's time and before, the concept of flying meshed or interlocked with the concept of the flier's awareness of flying—intending or meaning to fly, since the concept was first forged in the characterization of what birds, bats, and angels can do—all of them nonmechanical things. Thus it taxed the popular imagination to imagine an inanimate body flying. There was a genuine sense in which the concept of flying made it theoretically impossible that anything incapable of intending to fly (a machine) should be able to. And it taxed Leonardo's imagination likewise, to picture a contraption (a machine) which would go places somewhat as does a bird, without itself intending to. What distinguished his case from the popular was his ability to get the image of something "flying" (the scare-quotes are important) without flying, so he proceeded to make pictures and models under the guidance of the image. His imagination, in short, got to work, which meant he was conceiving something, thus *using* the pictures in the exploration and significant statement of the possibility that there be machines that can "fly." Notice that not for a moment did he wonder about such machines being able "inwardly" to want to fly, or about how to make *such* a machine—one that could fly and *mean* to. This to him would not have made sense, as it does not to us, despite what we say when we are just imaging and talking about possibilities under that spell.

I call "imagining" such a *use* of the imagination, distinguishing it "imaging" or image-mongering. There are other sorts of uses than this inventive one, as we will soon see. But the point here is that one can make sense with images under appropriate controls and in collaboration with concepts; and that such uses have a development and history, as in Leonardo's case. In *that* idiom, we have also imagined machines that can "talk English" (again, the scare-quotes) and have made most excellent ones, beginning with Edison's crude achievement. And we did not aim to make one which could "mean what it says;" nor, having made a "talking" machine, do we *really* think that *maybe* it does mean what it says, after all, though we have no reasons for believing it does. Not having any reasons for believing may occur in two logically different ways: for example, none of us has any reasons for believing that I shall die of heart failure in five minutes, though this is possible. In this case, we understand the hypothesis, and reject it on good grounds. But neither have you any reason for believing that a machine could talk and mean what it says. However, in this kind of case, there is neither acceptance nor rejection of a hypothesis, since none has been formulated. So there is not even a possibility question as in the first case. But you can imagine it? Imagine *what?* The point is that no possible or impossible state of affairs has been *formulated* for you either to imagine or fail to imagine, even after all the kaleidoscopic image-mongering or imaging that you indeed are able to engage in, under the conjuring spell of the words, but with no implications for what could or could not be the case.

It is the people I am addressing and rebuking who commonly will point to the airplane example—how incredible ("unimaginable") this was at first, etc.— as evidence that there could be machines which (now or eventually) can talk in the *bona fide* sense, *i.e.*, mean what they say, though this takes a greater stretch of the imagination, or that our intimate friends will turn out to be robots etc.— it all "could" happen. They would have a point if, in the airplane case, machines that intend to fly had been produced, or just cropped up and been discovered. Not even an approximation to "this state of affairs" (no state is described by these expressions, they are grammatical considerations) has been realized.

I have not talked enough about the verifiability-in-principle criterion of meaning in this connection, though I mentioned it earlier. What I have stressed so far is the tendency either to by-pass this standard, or only to *seem* to recognize it by asking, what can be *imaged?* (not imagined), and taking this as deciding what "could" be verified. It was this tendency that let the run-away camel into the tent of sense-making. This is all I am going to say here about verifiability and meaning, except to remind us that, after all, this concept is connected with that of *observation*, which is a very different thing from just imaging. Where the situation or purpose is scientific, the sense of "observe" is such that the truth of "S is observed to be P" warrants the inference that S *is* P. (This is a grammatical remark about the use of "observe.") And this involves conceptual controls on the mode of perception. This, in turn, means that if one is imagining a situation which would verify a statement, one would in effect be imagining a possible *observation*; and such imagining is also controlled by concepts, with educated respect for the objective meaning of the terms of the hypothesis. This is why the apparent sense of what looks like a hypothesis is not saved by a *deus ex machina* in the shape of another scatter-brained image, splattered into the picture just to keep the image-mongering going. The following would be a sort of test for whether this is going on or not; try to imagine a machine that talks and means it, then imagine it as just "talking" (without meaning it); is there any noticeable difference which would have any bearing on the question, could the machine really talk? If not, you are not *imagining* anything; just imaging, with no import for the question. And this imagery is spawned by the fact that you are not really doing anything with the expression, "can a talking machine mean what it says?" Here language is idling, and thought and genuine imagination are in abeyance. There is no real question. The upshot is that one can be in the throes of imaging without conceiving or imagining anything.

To bring out more clearly what "imagining" involves as distinguished from image-mongering, I proceed to a brief general account of it, under the head "image-management." Leonardo and the flying machine have given us a glimpse of it in one of its dimensions, namely, the inventive or technological. But there are two other general ways of managing images, all of which show the sense in which "imagining" is an achievement-word while "imaging" is not.

As a preliminary, let us notice a sense in which we can and do imagine objects as this or that. We will thereby discover what tempts people into their strange talk about what could be the case.

Look at Jastrow's duck-rabbit picture. This certainly can be *seen* as a rabbit or as a duck. Call these its "aspects," and keep in mind this special use of the term. I say "seen" advisedly because the seeing here is a mode of perception. If you cannot see the picture-object as a duck or a rabbit, you are aspect-blind. When you do see it, or when the aspect dawns, you wonder how you failed to see it; it is so plainly there to be seen. Yet, you hesitate to say the aspect is there to be observed, because there is something imaginative about the perception of the aspects, and the figure undergoes no observable change of qualities with the dawning of the aspect. It is as if you *see an image* in the medium of the picture, or the picture animated by the image. Call this mode of perception "prehension," distinguishing it from "observation." One "observes" that x is P, but one "prehends" x as y, where x is not y and y is an aspect of x animating it.

The crucial point for our concern is that for a given percipient prehending any x as y, or imagining x as y, makes sense only on the percipient's supposition that x is not y. Where x is y, we do not see it as *y* (say, a picture as a picture); we see that it is *y*. If you say that you see a cloud in the sky as a camel, you do not significantly at the same time suppose that the cloud could be a camel. (One does not see a cloud as a cloud, or a camel as a camel, but one as the other.) You may indeed falsely believe *that* the *x* up in the sky is a cloud; but imagining or prehending it as a camel—something all of us can do—will have no logical bearing whatsoever on the possibility of its being a camel. Any more than seeing the picture as a rabbit is any ground for supposing it could be one. The truth is that you can see it as a rabbit because you think it, the picture, is not one.

Now I suggest that this ability we all have to prehend things as things they are not, together with the fact that in such cases the image of what-the-object-is-not animates the object; it is this phenomenon, I suggest, that has misled us into supposing that things could be quite different from what *observation* of them would suggest. In our talking machine case, we can indeed see it as an angular sort of human being; an aspect of consciousness dawns and animates the robot—an image of something alive. It is for the sake of such dramatic prehensions that some science fiction and moving pictures are produced, without the slightest bearing on the question of even the possibility of there being such creatures or of making them. Again here, this prehensive or imaginative experience presupposes that these *x's* are *not* conscious, insofar as they are being seen "as conscious."

Now, this capacity for prehension—imaginatively seeing things as things they are not for observation—has been harnessed in wonderful ways. The trouble resulted not from it *per se* but only from misconstruing or confusing its functions. In general, there are three of these, displayed by (1) the technologist, (2) the artist, and (3) the theorist.

When the technologist wants, like Leonardo, to invent something—to fly with, to travel in, to compute with—he sees (imagines) the appropriate material he is going to work with *as* the desired instrument. Such imagining will pay respect to various things that have been observed to be, or are known to be, the case. Then, under the guidance of this image, he manipulates the material till the image is realized in it and the product (invention) is ready for the experimental test. From the beginning, the image will be portrayable in pictures and models; these will be the direct expression of the image and do its work of guiding the operation. Of course, the result, in this technological case, is for use as an instrument, so, once it is constructed, it will cease to be the occasion for a continued prehensive looking at it.

It is the art-object that is brought into being for the sake of a refined prehension itself. The artist gets an imaginative impression of something, an image, then manipulates his medium to express the image, suffused with emotion. Such manipulation is a deliberate and technical operation as in the case of the technologist, but it is for the sake of the beholder's seeing the composition as something that it is not. The image of this something "animates" the work, which thus expressively portrays the artist's impression—brings it to the prehensive view of the beholder.

In its theoretical function, prehension is closely allied with observation, as scientific (*scientia*) imagination. It then subserves the kind of looking that yields hypotheses, descriptive and explanatory, covering the nature of things. The aim of imagination in this exercise is not primarily to introduce into the situation what was not there in the state of nature, as in the other two cases; though it remains prehensive insofar as it sees certain things ("causes") as they *might* not be, subject to eventual check by observations. But its main aim is to imagine an observation which would supply a check for a theory whose concepts make the demand, and determine what observation will count. The observation not yet made may require delicate instruments, and in the invention of these devices, imagination operates technologically as in the first case bringing something into being, constructing it. *Any significant claim that something "maybe" is thus-and-so will be made in this framework* of theorizing. Likewise, the sense of the expression "what can be imagined," where the question has this theoretical import, is illustrated by, say, the difference between the little scientists who could not imagine the experimental observation that would decide whether light rays bend in passing through the strong gravitational field near the sun, and the great scientists who could. This sense of what can be imagined is *not* illustrated by imagining, say, the sun's personal charm as attracting the light rays towards it, in full view of the smiling moon. This in the context would be *imaging*, not imagining, and has no bearing on even what "maybe" is the case; since no theoretically significant conception even of what *might* be the case accompanies the image. In this light, nothing about the sun has been said which could be even "highly improbable." You need a proposition for that. And if you add, but at least it is *logically* possible, the answer is that we cannot say whether the expression is logically possible or not, because, in it, concepts have collapsed into sheer images, and contradiction is a relation between concepts. Yours is a case of image-mongering.

Yet you will say, surely, the expression is not sheer nonsense, it does have a meaning. I am prepared to concede this, but please attend carefully to the proviso. It involves what might be called an aspect-theory of the meaning of some verbal expressions. Suppose you have an image in mind — again the sun being winsome toward the starlight passing it, you could even draw a picture exhibiting or expressing the image as in a cartoon — well, suppose you have this image and you then express it in the above *verbal* way. Now I get to the delicate point. Just as by looking at your pencil sketch, I "get" the image, by seeing the picture *as* the coy sun (prehension); so I may get or prehend the same image in the medium of the spoken words, the verbal sketch. In fact, many expressions are commonly "understood" in this way — they express images that we prehend in the expression. Of course, you must know the language to have this experience of pictorial meaning. The living language is radiant or gravid with it. And the literary artist, the poet, is skillful as a specialist in detecting this, and managing the verbal medium in a way that animates it with fine images, suffused with emotion; a way that shows that this rhythmic idiom is plainly not a statement of what might some day be *observed* to be the case—not even of what is logically possible or impossible. *These* are concepts for another kind of formulation, with a different sort of sense.

"Theorizing," or "theory-construction," has, however, a broader import, recognition of which requires me to moderate my strong statement tying all theory to an observational base. There is a myth-making or epic-making use of language which is more for the sake of expressing cosmic images of things, to be prehended in, say, a metaphysics or a theology. Such expressions may be the occasion to see something in things, with the force of a revelation. They *show* us something which the scientific idiom cannot, or in a way in which that language does not. Sometimes what cannot be *said* that way can be *shown* in another. Much more needs to be said detailing the nature of this prehensive perception and its language, but that is another story.

I get back, in the end, to the series of questions I began with, about what could talk. There is a final point to be made about the increasing perplexity, from the first to the last. My text, with this in view, is from Wittgenstein: "A smiling mouth *smiles* only in a human face." Anywhere else there is only "smiling." He might have said the same thing about talking; a talking mouth *talks* only in a human face. (The Cheshire cat did not smile; hyenas do not laugh; does a bird *sing*?) Now, Wittgenstein would admit that we can see (prehend) these creatures *as* doing these things. But where the question concerns what it *is* they are or could be doing, we need scare-quotes for some of the cases. The Japanese ten-year-old indeed could talk English. The human imbecile? Maybe, with certain provisos. The parrot parrots English; it could not talk it—this is a grammatical remark about the relation of concepts. Still, it has a mouth, one which can form sounds, recognizable as English words on human lips; perhaps it can intend to produce them, but we do not know what it would be like for it to mean what it says; if it can do this, it can silently think what it is going to say; the concepts go together. Our concept of this capacity breaks down here in the parroting English case. It is a bit worse in the lion's case because here not only is the "talking" mouth out of place; we hear nothing *like* English proceeding from it—yet in other respects the lion is more like us than a parrot; it is not a bird. The machine's case really bothers us because, though it has a hole on top, it is not alive like the parrot and the lion. We feel better about talking or just "talking" which is accompanied by some feelings and sensations. Then, in the cases after this, we do not even have anything like a mouth. The *conception* we are wondering about is here completely drained from the very *question* of what could be the case.

The general point here is that for something to be expressive or meaningful, it must be in the right place. This is a sort of situational theory of meaning. (We already have an ethics of situation.) Our concepts take shape in the situation of their use, where they have been forged for these uses, and this leaves them with what Waismann has called "open texture," in view of the way in which, say, the mouth belongs with the face, the face with the rest of the human being in human action, in the situation. When all these are in the "right place," the face may light up with a smile which is expressive, not only of merriment or friendship, but the whole character of the person. Thus also does the concept of talking interlock with others. It merges with them, and breaks down or is dissolved in isolation from them. So we mist be careful with such concepts as those of smiling or talking, since in some applications they collapse, leaving only images for image-mongering.

Yet, perhaps even image-mongering has a certain value. It has no *guidance*-value. It does not formulate what is or could be the case. But it may *goad* us into an awareness of the limits which our language is placing upon our powers of expression. The criteria being what they are, we can make sense in this way and not in that. But the image-mongering suggests (without saying) that these rules are not immutable imperatives writ large in the sky. This final remark itself, however, will probably *goad* us more than it will *guide* us. Here I leave the matter in your charge.

18.

This notion of "gauging with the eye," what does it involve? I have seen wild mountain goats in the Himalayas hesitate a moment before leaping from rock to rock on the face of the precipice, and a sparrow hawk poise in the sky before diving on a field mouse. And Pender, my Siamese cat, will strain upwards with her eyes at the open drawer three feet above while her whole body beneath; adjusts for action, before making the upward leap. Did they all gauge distances with their eyes? Were they giving things a measuring look?

One does not confidently say yes, because of the influence of another model for gauging with the eye, a human one. Here, the notion savors of engineering. In fact, gauging with the eye in this sense is the preliminary part of a constructive operation upon something. Seeing an area of the field of experience this way, one is preparing to modify something in it. In short, the intention of such seeing is to bring about a change in its object, and an artifact into existence. It is a looking that organizes the seer or agent for an operation, constructive or destructive, upon the object. This is what distinguishes it from the above animal uses of the eyes, the purpose of which is not the invention of something, but, rather simply the appropriation by the agent of what is already there. Such vision simply directs the seer towards such appropriations.

Both sorts of seeing, however, maintain a practical relation to things. But the interesting point to notice here is how the human gauging with the eye nevertheless differs from animal seeing. Bent as it is on making artifacts, it must schematize a space in which things are ordered to appear as physical objects. The early Egyptian surveyors were called "rope stretchers" because they gave the terrain on which there was to be a construction a sort of visible metrics by stretching ropes aver it. It then took on a determinate metrics in the reference-frame of which the constructive operation could be performed. As the eye became educated for such seeing, it could gauge things in that sort of space without the help of the ropes that gave it a definite tri-dimensionality. This structural feature of things in a determinate kind of space does not belong to them in the Ur-space in which animals see and move. In short, things are encountered simply as things in the field of animal experience, not as "objects." To be an object, a thing must make an exclusive sort of appearance in a space that has become determinate in a special way of looking. In this sense, the human "gauging with the eye" is more "objective" than animal vision, meaning that, thus viewed, things appear as physical objects, as they do not in animal perception. And this sets the stage for the operations of technological intelligence.

It is this notion of operation, together with construction, that has been the keynote of twentieth-century philosophy and methodology of science. The "operationalism" of Bridgman, for example, is the theory that the very concepts of science are defined by the sorts of operations that are performed in determining whether or not they apply. "Length" or "distance," for example. You know what "diameter of the earth" means in proportion as you have some idea of what to do to ascertain the earth's diameter. Such concepts can therefore be more or less vague. "Diameter of the whole universe" and "the universe's origin" are relatively vague concepts at present even for the most advanced scientists, because they have such a vague idea of the operational procedures that would determine the answers to questions in which these expressions occur. So the very questions border on being "pseudo." They don't quite make sense. Of course, as progress is made in the conception of such operations, and experimental devices invented for carrying them out, the questions become more and more *bona fide*. Before this happens, however, it is mostly pictures or images that accompany the questions, deceiving the less sophisticated people into thinking that they make sense because they mistake the imagery for their meaning. So these people are left with the impression that the questions are meaningful without the operational controls on the thinking about them. The logical positivists supported the operationalists in cautioning people against such a mistake, though their theory took the form of "constructionism." The pictorial and emotive functions of the ordinary language we live by in our more personal dealings with things are to be purged out of the language of science by "constructing" this into an artificial, well-formed idiom that protects the scientific thinker against "non-cognitive" influences from life and its "natural" language, in favor of the physical objects of cognitively concerned experience (observation) and thought. Such "physicalism," however, was distinguished by the foremost logical positivists Neurath and Carnap—from materialism of the old metaphysical variety. Their point was fundamentally a logical and methodological one about how to make "cognitive sense," which for them is the exclusive function of science. Any *bona fide* bit of knowledge about anything is to be arrived at only under such controls, keeping the concepts of the discipline in clear logical relations to one another, while keeping the whole conceptual superstructure of the theory based on the "observation sentences" that tie it down to matters of fact.

Now, with this distinction between meaning and image in view, the meaning alone being operationally determined, an important point can be made about the history of scientific thought. The common failure to notice it has resulted in a mistake that has become almost standard. It is commonly asserted that the ancient Greeks were the first atomists. This is true only if the crucial methodological distinction I have in mind is glossed over. Here is the distinction; the Greeks, specifically Democritus and Leucippus, were picture-thinkers. Their thinking about the nature of things was not sufficiently under the operational-experimental controls that distinguish scientific thought from philosophical thought. The method of the latter permits it to be more speculative. "Speculative" is connected with the Latin "speculum," meaning "mirror." This suggests mirror-image and, as a matter of fact, the speculative mind of philosophy has frequently itself been pictured as an inner mirror mirroring the external world. A book has appeared in my own century called *Speculum Mentis*, by Collingwood. Well, my point is that scientific thought has now emerged from the matrix, finally showing its distinctive nature that, as embryonic, was obscured in the amalgam of early speculative or philosophical thought. And the early atomism was generated more by picture-thinking than by operational thinking about the ultimate constituents of matter. Atoms were pictured, not operationally conceived. This means that they were taken to be little bits of the stuff of the things of which we have perceptual images.

It is against such picture-thinking in physics that twentieth century scientists have taken a stand. In short, the revolution in science that we associate with relativity and quantum theory is primarily a methodological one, a systematic attempt to get away from the pictorial elements that denatured science even in the classical physics of Newton. As one German scientist puts it, scientists now realize that a scientific theory cannot be supported by an appeal to "Anschaulichkeit," where this means intuition of pictorial elements, howsoever sublime the impact of these may be on speculative thought.

Another scientist calls this leaning on picture-models the disease of "modelitis."

Maybe this makes it clear why I am disinclined to say that atomism began with the Greeks. But my remarks also show the sort of relation *scientific* atomism has with the earlier, more speculative sort that included non-scientific ingredients.

19.

Whether color-words can be operationally defined is still a moot question. But if a color is construed as a property of a physical object, the concept of it does have *some* connection with operational procedures. Several years ago I brought this out in a little essay called "Colors as Universals." Since this got noticed by a number of people working in optical laboratories, I present it here in relation to technology.

Colors As Universals

Arguments seesaw around the "locus" of color, if any, whether one and the same color can be in several places at once, and all this has something to do with the question of colors as universals. The tendency is to call a color a universal if it can be thought of either as nowhere in space at all, or as capable of being in a number of places at once without being in the intervening spaces. Those who hold that both these alternatives are false are generally the nominalists, the disbelievers in colors as universals. They will commonly have a concept of generality, but this will be something belonging in some way to general *terms* whose function is to denote ambiguously any member of classes of more or less similar colors. And they will try to show that the analysis of similarity or classes does not involve or disclose a covert universality.

Perhaps one way to start arbitrating such a dispute, both sides of which have something on the ball, is to bring up the method of operational definition and give it a special twist. Speaking of balls, let's use one as an illustration. If I should say that this croquet ball is near the center of the lawn, perhaps a glance would suffice to confirm my statement, but what gives the looking confirmatory power is the incipient awareness of certain operations (measuring with a stick) which I visualize as I look, without the actual measuring performance. It is this that makes the glance a knowing one and a kind of confirmation. (Of course, there is another way to put this: I gauge distances with my eye; but such gauging and distances involve association with units of length represented by footrulers or yardsticks, etc. The incipient visualizing of these laid end to end gives the looking its cognitive force.) At any rate, you can see that the ball is near the center thanks at least to *some* practices (if not the end-to-end ones) the "sense" of which is incorporated into the seeing. So, we say of such a statement about the locus—the situation, the place—of the croquet ball, that it not only makes cognitive sense but is true.

Suppose, next, that I should say that the paint of the croquet ball is on its surface. It may seem that, if this is to be a *bona fide* location, we must make sure first that we can locate the surface. We must know where it is. Shall we say that the surface of the ball is on it? This sounds a little silly. The ball doubtless has a surface, and there is paint on the surface, but where is the surface? Having raised this profound question I want to postpone answering it till after I have located the paint. The answer then will be more intelligible.

To say that the paint is on the surface of the ball seems to be significant and true, again because of the incipient awareness of certain operations that have been or might be performed, namely, the laying it on with a brush or the scraping it off after the application of paint remover. Somehow or other, this gives the paint itself the status of a substance or thing, like the croquet balls, and that is why it is readily located. You can significantly say (truly or falsely) where it is. It is an at-least-three-dimensional thing. This cannot be said of the surface of the ball. A surface is not a thing or substance. It is the boundary between contiguous things, hence *itself* cannot significantly be said to be anywhere. A correct analysis shows, therefore, that, when I say the paint is on the surface of the ball, I am saying that the ball and the paint are contiguous in a special way. I am not locating the surface, but the ball in relation to the paint. The surface per se remains unlocated and unlocatable. People feel compelled to think of the surface as itself somehow on or coating the ball precisely because they picture it as a sort of thin peel which a fine enough razor blade might remove. So they imagine it as between the paint and the ball like an undercoating. But, upon second thought, it is plain that surfaces are not like that. Only potato peeling and paint and the like are, and these *have* surfaces but certainly *are* not surfaces. You may have layer upon later of coats of paint but not of surfaces. And if we speak significantly of outer and inner surfaces, we are using an ellipsis for one thing (say, paint) cover-another thing (say, ball) each of which has its own surface. The outer surface does not, strictly speaking, cover the inner one.

But I want to move on to the main point, about color. I have located the ball and I have located its paint. Finally, suppose I say that the color (red) of the paint is on the surface of the paint. It may seem at first that what I am saying here is logically isomorphic with my statement about the paint being on the surface of the ball. That is, the color seems to stand to the paint as the paint stands to the ball. As the paint is on the surface of the ball, so the red may seem to be on the surface of the paint. But let us get busy with some more operational analysis, to find out what I am saying if anything. Can I scrape the color off the paint, as I can the paint off the ball? Or, by what operations if any is the red put on to the paint? Is the paint painted with a red color as the ball was painted with a red paint? A little reflection shows that colors are not laid on with brushes. Paints are. People sometimes tell artists that they put certain colors in the wrong place in the picture. But this again is an ellipsis. They mean that certain paints were put in the wrong place, and the ensuing color scheme was unfortunate. They allow themselves this laxness of speech again because, unawares, they picture the color itself as a fine peel, as they misconstrued the surface. The red lies on the paint as the paint lies on the ball, they think.

I can, by looking, see where the ball is, and where its paint is. These glances were made knowing by incorporating the sense of certain practices or operations, which give the ball and the paint the status of movable and removable things. Thus they have positions in space (and time). Can I, by looking, similarly see where the color is? It is so easy and natural to say that I see it on the surface of the paint, and that seems to locate it with the paint, contiguously. But we have noticed that what makes it possible to see where the paint and the ball are (the operations) tends to be absent from the vision of color pure and simple. You can remove paint from the painted object and carry the paint from one place to another, but you cannot remove the color and carry it around while leaving the paint behind. That is why it may be said, operationally speaking, that it makes sense to talk about the position of the paint but not of the color. You cannot even say significantly that the color "moves with" the moving paint or object, as "the mind" cannot significantly be said to go along with the body during a trip, or not to go along.

Perhaps some of the classical philosophers, including Plato, were operational thinkers without knowing it. The Platonists especially should like the results of this operational analysis of the alleged locations of color. It is a sort of justification of the vague notion that at least some qualities are nowhere in space and therefore universal. This leads on to the assertion that there are universals, the thesis of logical realism.

But the justification that operationalism gives this thesis is underhanded. Classical realism needs considerable pruning, or expurgating. When the operationalist says that you cannot move a color around, he does not interpret this as implying that there are entities outside space. He notices that this is a picturesque expression ("outside space," etc.) itself failing to make straightforward congitive sense by the operational criterion. In short, it is misleading. It misleads some people into supposing that since colors are not here in space, they must be somewhere else, namely, outside it. (A book was recently published called *Behind the Universe*.) What analysis reveals is not this, but simply that terms ordinarily designating spatial position lose their (cognitive) sense in conjunction with pure color predicates. This entails only that the assertion that color is somewhere and it's contradictory that it is nowhere, both fail to say anything cognitively significant—they are neither true nor false. So logical realism, if to be identified with the contradictory, is to be rejected as a misleading *maniere de parler*. "You cannot move a color around" would seem to entail that you cannot budge a color, and this seems to be an expression of the same logical type as "You cannot budge the Rock of Gibraltar." Actually, it is like saying that you cannot budge the universe, a very different kind of expression. This does not characterize anything truly or falsely. When people talk this way, they probably have dimly in view something else that is indeed a fact, namely, that the term "budge" or "move" in connection with "the whole universe" collapses into cognitive nonsense, howsoever significant it may continue to be in a pictorial way. That is why you "cannot budge the universe" — or a color.

It may at first occur to someone that colors *can* be made to move, even dance around, by, say, pressing eyeballs. But, on second thought, it becomes clear that the reference here is *not* to the color of a thing, but to some *appearance* of it and the thing — an appearance under possible correction and controls.

It would be important and interesting to find out what other quality predicates, besides the pure color ones, behave like the color predicates. (We have already noticed that "surface" does.) The extended examination might clarify and confirm, by a more adequate formulation, the recurrent philosophical impression that only things or substances or events are "particulars," while qualities or attributes *as such* have a sort of nowhereness about them which has been captured in the concept of "universal." A more empirical tradition, such as influenced Kant, would put the matter differently. The empirical qualities-as-such are, in this view, not universals but the unformed sensory material of a given manifold, the data of pure experience. There is the same nowhereness about data on a subconceptual or subformal level as seems to characterize universals, since data take on definite spatio-temporal character including position only as elements *conceived* as the organized clusters of properties "belonging to" intelligible things.

A final question, which to me is always a puzzler: Why is the conjunction of pure color predicates with position designators so productive of nonsense? Isn't it because colors, *an und für sich*, simply do not have spatial positions? My impression is that this is like asking, doesn't "budge" in conjunction with "the whole universe" make nonsense simply because the universe is unbudgable? Clearly, if one could significantly and truly say that the universe is an immovable object, then the expression, "you can budge the universe," would be false, not nonsense, and its contradictory would be true. But I am in a muddle about such questions at bottom, especially as applied to colors. My trouble is that, on the one hand, it seems to me that one should be able to "see" whether colors are nowhere or somewhere, by a kind of inspection of them. On the other hand, I find the result of the operational analysis above convincing and so incline to the conclusion that expressions attempting to locate, or deny location to, colors are cognitively nonsensical. It may be that my difficulty is a latent dissatisfaction with operationalism. Perhaps I can understand and know expressions about color positions in space without operational controls or definitions. But I have yet to be convinced of the superiority of such a view.

20.

Twentieth-century scientists realize that a scientist thinks with his instruments of experiment and discovery, and how this influences and educates even the way he *perceives* things. (See R. N. Hanson's book on this theme.) It was the lack of refined instruments for exploring microscopic and extraordinarily large phenomena that left the Greek cosmologist unaware of the prevalence of images in his thought, and of the operational character of scientific thinking.

The fact that scientists employ instruments to make their operational thinking more penetrating into the nature of things as physical objects tempts some people to make the mistake of supposing that such science is "practical" and that these scientists are moved by practical concerns. This is to over-look a crucial distinction between "applied" and "practical." Consider the following set of sub-divisions:

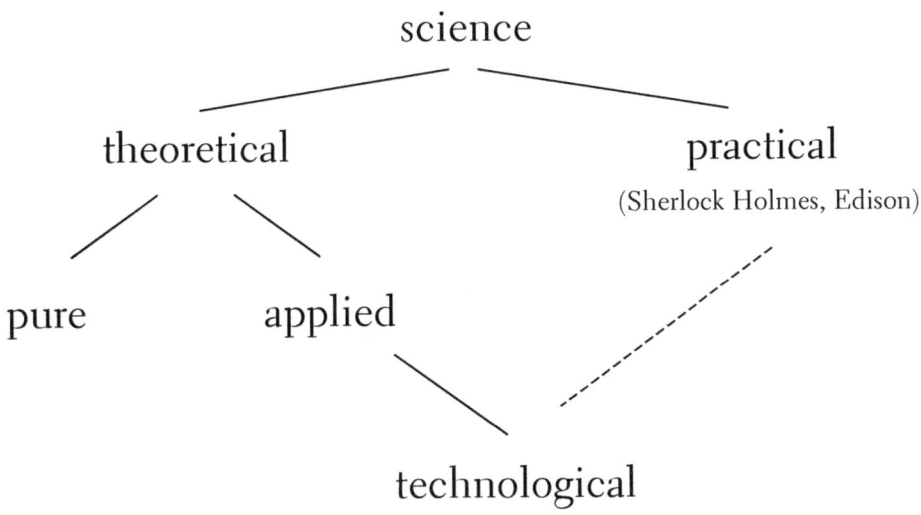

"Practical" here stands in opposition to "theoretical," while "applied" is a sub-division under "theoretical." The failure of many people to make the distinctions this way infuriates the applied scientist, since it makes it look as if he, like Edison, is concerned to get along with as little theory as possible. Or like Sherlock Holmes, who was a genius at finding out particular matters of fact by putting two and two together, without "applying" any general theory to anything for the sake of the confirmation. Taking "science" in its stricter sense, as procedure aimed at general knowledge for its own sake, Holmes and Edison were not scientists at all, not even applied scientists. The applied *scientist* seeks to formulate a law under which certain phenomena are regularly connected, and that therefore has an explanatory power not confined to a particular situation. He does not seek the particular cause of a given particular effect (Holmes), nor does he seek to produce a certain particular effect from a given particular cause (Edison). Except to get evidence for a theory. Rather, the applied scientist wants to explain the causal connection between those *sorts* of states of affairs, or why those sorts of things go so regularly together. (Why, e.g., the vacuum and the brilliant tungsten wire go so constantly together.)

What gives him the air of being "practical" is that, in order to force nature to answer such questions, he must use experimental set-ups and this requires the production of instruments—certain devices he must make. The making of these gives him the appearance of being practically concerned. But, unlike the practical man, he makes things for the sake of something he wants to know with their help. Whereas the practical man makes things for the sake of other things he wants to make, until in the end he reaches the satisfaction of some non-theoretical or "practical" interest. Edison made tungsten wire, etc., so he could make a light bulb, so people could switch light on in dark places, so they could see, so they could get on with their end-of-the-day affairs without the inconvenience of cleaning, filling, and applying matches to, kerosene lamps. Edison was a genius at this sort of thing. But, since he did not make, say, the phonograph to be used as an aid to a more penetrating look into the nature of something else, it was not part of an experimental set-up, and he was not therefore an applied scientist. An applied scientist uses his artifacts as instruments for finding out whether what his *theory* says about something is true. What he is applying, with the help of his mechanical inventions, is a theory. And this is why we don't simply call him a great "inventor" like Edison. He is, after all, a theorist. "Inventor" is usually reserved for the man who is good at producing instruments upon demand without himself being primarily motivated by a theoretical interest bent upon confirmation of hypotheses.

This brings me to "technologist." Was Edison a technologist? I, for one, feel hesitant to answer affirmatively, though I am guilty of having used "technological intelligence" in the looser and larger sense. And there is a sufficient reason for the hesitation. The technologist, strictly speaking, has a considerable knowledge of theories that he, *qua* technologist, has inherited or acquired, not himself discovered and formulated. It is working this way with scientific theories that distinguishes his ilk from that of Edison. He is good not only at invention, but at achieving this with the help of an appreciable body of scientific knowledge. But he is similar to the simple inventor like Edison with respect to doing his work without himself, as a technologist, tending to prove a theory thereby. But, as a technologist and not as a simple inventor, he *may* be assigned the job of inventing experimental apparatus which can be used by the applied scientist for theoretical purposes (confirmation of a hypothesis, etc). So the technologist is in a better position to collaborate with the theoretical scientist than is the simple inventor without much knowledge of science. Still, if you count heads, it turns out that a majority of technologists are employed as servants of practical interests. It is these "scientists"—this must be put in quotes, used thus—who do not feel the exhilaration of being close to the pioneering work of the theoretical scientists.

Here is a sort of gamut that illustrates the distinctions I have been making: the "pure" scientist at one end, let us say Riemann with his non-Euclidean geometry. The "impure" or applied scientist, say Max Planck with his quantum theory experimentally evidenced. Both these are "theoretical" scientists. Between these comes a significant intermediate sort of case such as Einstein's, with his Relativity theory which is a kind of non-Euclidean geometry given an interpretation that confers "physical meaning" upon it, making it "applicable." But Einstein himself had little to do with devising the experimental apparatus that established the theory by making it possible to detect the bending of light rays in passing the sun. So he is a cross between the pure and the impure scientist, but certainly a theoretical scientist since both sorts are such. Then comes the technologist who is conversant with scientific theories but whose main purpose is not himself to formulate and test these, rather to use them in the construction of physical devices that may be used by people either for theoretical purposes or for the satisfaction of practical interests. This involves some inventiveness and the constructions are inventions, but the technologist is not "simply" an inventor, owing to his rapport with theories. Finally, at the other end of the gamut, is the "practical" inventor of useful articles, like Edison, who "simply" invents. Francis Bacon called these the "empirics," whose giftedness is mainly an affair of what I shall call "physical imagination," not the power of intellectual grasp of principles. This is the earmark of the practical scientist. Technological intelligence is certainly at work here also, but in the older sense of the Greek root of the term, "*technē*," or of the Sanskrit "*taksh*," meaning the practical art of shaping, cutting or making, akin to the art of the carpenter. In my twentieth century, the intelligence called technological has a closer alliance with science proper, meaning theoretical science. Thus, if the practical emphasis is the main thing, we now feel inclined to call what follows "technology" and "science" in those shudder-quotes. Not technology and science proper. What we then have is practical know-how. It is worth noticing that, in the aristocratic mind of the Greeks, even the making and using of experimental apparatus was associated with technology in this practical know-how sense, and so was looked down upon as a manual skill beneath the dignity of the scientist proper. It was Francis Bacon who, contemplating the scientific practices especially of Harvey and Galileo, imported working with instruments into science as a fundamental part of sound theorizing. In short, the intellectual aristocracy of the Greeks disinclined the best of them to operate as applied scientists, making their concept of science formal and deductive. But not till the beginning of my twentieth century was the true import of this driven home, by the pictureless thinking with instruments in relativity and quantum physics. This was the true methodological revolution that took the pictorial or "speculative" elements out of Newtonian cosmology, replacing it with theories that made operational sense.

Surely it is clear from the way I have made all these distinctions between "theoretical," "technological," and the rest, that it is quite possible for the *same* man to combine some or all of the distinct functions and even to be rather good at each. Usually, however, the man who is a real winner in one of these games, a genius at it in this age of specialization, will not excel in many of the others. He will be a specialist. But, even then, excellent though he is at, say, the metrics and dynamics of moving bodies like Galileo, he may also have the inventive technological intelligence to make the first telescope—to prove a theory.

21.

Does metaphysical materialism follow from the triumphs of twentieth-century natural science and technology? The metaphysical materialist maintains such propositions as, the ultimate stuff of all things, including minds, is matter, or, everything is material. Well, it is just such expressions that the logic of recent science holds up as senseless. They are not propositions at all, since a proposition is true or false and confirmable or testable. "Everything is material" together with its opposite, "Everything is spiritual"—the thesis of a spiritualistic metaphysics—are precisely the sort of expressions for which science as such has no use; they never occur in science proper. The current scientist tends to call these bits of metaphysics, "metaphysics" here meaning "senseless," and he will have nothing to do with them since they are neither confirmable nor disconfirmable by the operational procedures of science, in thought and experimental action. The influence here is that of logical positivism, with its theory of meaning.

Even Bertrand Russell, who has been a metaphysical materialist off and on, says that modern physics has resulted in the disappearance of matter "as a thing" (his *ABC of Atoms*). This can be interpreted as denying that matter is a stuff, but the main point of such remarks as Russell's is usually that matter has been discovered to be "energy" instead of inert bits of "stuff." This has been the unfortunate occasion for too many theologians and metaphysicians inclined toward spiritualism to argue that even physical science is now demonstrating the spirituality of all things. It has long been a tradition in classical philosophy to suppose that anything really active or energetic is mental or spiritual, since material substance is by definition inert stuff. Bishop Berkeley, for example. But this is to overlook the sharp distinction between the concepts of physical and spiritual energy. An exploding hydrogen bomb exhibits the former nicely. Beethoven, continuing fiercely to compose great music right to the end even after becoming stone deaf, is exhibit number one of the latter. Surely these are very different things, even in essence if you want to press it that way. Even if you truly say that matter is radiant energy in essence, you are working here with a physical concept. The "radiant energy" of a Beethoven or of a Beethovenesque composition is a very different concept, a spiritual one. To argue that there is a common essence and a spiritual one in the two cases because "energy" is used in both, is like arguing that because both a piece of metal and Beethoven become fatigued—"fatigue" applies also to a steel spring—there must be something mental or spiritual in essence about both. Which would be to overlook the very different concepts that go along with the word "fatigue," its variety of uses.

22.

Assignment for the technologist: let a hundred million people listen simultaneously in the privacy of their homes to the beating of a man's heart and simultaneously see a cardiograph recording it, and let the hearing and the seeing be more adequate than they would be if each were to press his ear against the man's chest or be standing in the room containing the cardiograph. Moreover, let the man be a hundred and fifty miles out in space orbiting the earth at seventeen thousand five hundred miles an hour while this is going on.

At the beginning of my century, even three decades into it when I was nearly thirty years old, such an assignment would have raised a scream of outrage and a howl of derision. In those days, around the world in eighty days was a feat. Several months ago, I heard and saw astronaut John Glenn's heart, in satisfaction of the above assignment. Around the world in eighty minutes. Something in me dissolved in wonder and fear as I had that experience. Technology is wonderful. And fearful.

This reminds me of God, who is both wonderful and fearful. And this, in turn, reminds me again of Rilke whose notion of "thing" versus "object" I have already touched on. It is his notion of God this time that intrigues me. According to Rilke's informal theology, God is being slowly realized or coming into being only in and through certain accomplishments of human beings, who themselves become divine in that part of the process that creates God. Nietzsche had a similar notion toward the end of the last century and, not long after the turn into my century, the British philosopher Samuel Alexander built the idea up into a speculative cosmology, giving God the last place in time as the final Emergent but the first and highest place in the scheme of values.

I wonder if there is any sense in which the awful and fearful power of the emerging and still infant technology is a manifestation of God coming into being? One is inclined to both worship and tremble before it. Many people are idolizing it, individually and by institutional enactment. Of course, anyone suggesting this sort of thing would have to face the objection that it could be the Devil that is putting on the show in the act of self-realization, aiming at the eventual destruction of mankind. How is one to decide? Is it God thundering in nuclear explosion and sonic boom, or is it the Devil? One could by-pass the issue by rejecting both alternatives, and this is just what most people do because they take the idea as a literal one. But if you respond to it as you would to a myth, you feel yourself up against a real problem that requires considerable unsnarling. You remember analogous cases where there is a sort of meeting of extremes at bottom; love and hate, laughing and crying, pain and pleasure, good and evil. And you wonder if God and the Devil are similarly related, on a foundation of something more ultimate than either, in one relation to which man is blessed and in another damned. The most advanced theology of my century, Paul Tillich's, is best understood if approached with some such idea in mind, as we shall see later.

All these speculations would jar Rilke. His God is realized in an inner, childlike, elemental condition of creative solitude, where "elemental" is associated with his poetic concept of a thing embedded in unspoiled nature, as distinguished from an object. This ideal is as far from that of the outward and powerful pyrotechnics of twentieth-century technology as one can get—God without sonic thunder, one whose human creators tend to live out their lives in quiet desperation, the circumstances being what they are. It is these Rilkes and Thoreaus who are worried about the gradual replacement of natural community of things by the strident collectivity of objects under the general laws that technological intelligence is framing. My impression is that what they have in view may be suggested as follows: as the sense of the earthy community or intimacy of things with one another wanes in the technological view of them as physical objects, so the sense of personal community among people is also waning as the technological consciousness of their dependence on collectivization under law grows. The political consciousness of the twentieth century has this new complexion or content, and all this illustrates what I meant by "technological determinism." Things and people fall within its scope. And relations become more and more impersonal or simply less intimate *on principle*, even obligatory, as such collectivity preempts the area of community. . . .

Up to forty years ago, I could still buy a horse and buggy. Up to five years ago, I could get the make of car I like without power brakes and power steering. Today I must get these powered. The option is gone. So now I just go places fast and efficiently. I do not go driving or for a drive. And the trouble is that I shall probably prefer the latest automations when I get used to them, as I have long preferred my car to a horse and buggy. That is another and a more direct illustration of what I meant by technological determinism. Things get progressively automated; so does the activity of people along with them, by their having to string along with the process, called "progress." And progress it is, with a vengeance, technologically speaking. But men have also been in the right relation to technological power, in which it has blessed him even as a human being. What the controls are on this must be looked at more closely, sooner or later.

23.

The Impressions I have had of twentieth-century socio-political developments are now beginning to form a cluster, demanding the center of attention that science and technology have held hitherto in these reflections. The transition feels natural, since my impressions of even the latter have from the first been reeking with implications for social and political theory. So much so that I have already had to spell some of these out. If I were doing an academic essay I would have to apologise for the way my impressions keep fusing across topical demarcations. But I am either just thinking in a game of verbal solitaire or conversing with an imaginary company of just people. (I almost said "audience" instead of "company" under the influence of the professional sclerosis I'm trying here to limber myself out of, before I die.) People are not professional academicians. And conversely. I mean that professional academicians are not people. You can add "as such" if you like, for academic reasons. (The point of "Professional academicians as such are not people" is like the point of "Physical objects as such are not things." People and things have something more meaty about them. Their appearance as academicians and physical objects is more skeletal. Remember, however, that basically it is things and people that are appearing under these emaciated forms, with the density of the originals left out.)

24.

I have been making it look as if political consciousness, with its minimizing of relations of personal and spontaneous intimacy, is a function of the advance of technology. But surely people were politically conscious before this snowballing development in the twentieth century. And were not they huddled together in lonely crowds before, regimented by external power with authority to regulate the society? Even Plato wrote of the lack of genuine community in a state run by a tyrannical government. And his follower Plotinus set the pace for subsequent mysticism by his famous emphasis on the loneliness of the human soul in its ultimate condition of being "alone with the Alone." In view of such antecedents, can the notion be justified that the currently mushrooming technology has any special relation, a determining one, to twentieth-century political consciousness and the aloneness of individuals caught in it?

Yes, it can be justified by several considerations but especially by a closer look at French existentialism. The philosophy of Jean Paul Sartre key-notes something characteristic of my century. It is on this that I want to dwell here. Since his thought takes both a philosophical and a dramatic turn, it exhibits what I have in view in different modes of expression and has therefore been influential outside philosophy proper. This makes it even more relevant to the improper sort of philosophy I'm doing.

The first step in the approach to what existentialism key-notes is to show how it differs from the classical antecedents mentioned above. According to Sartre, the aloneness of the individual is desperate because it is built in. There is no escape from it into genuine community with *anything*. He puts this technically by saying that there is no essence that the individual shares with anything else. This is not only to say that the individual is unique—most philosophers have said this without denying essential community—but it stresses the radical point that any coherent system whose elements cooperate as members of the same community is a fiction or figment created by fiat. One has to will order into being if one is to have an ordered world to live in, and even then the community he lives, moves, and has his being in has no ontological sanction, meaning that it does not rest on any foundation that was objectively there to accommodate it beforehand. Strictly speaking, there are no objective requirements to be satisfied in the willful process of constructing a community. You create it by sustained will-power. And you do this desperately because you feel all along that the only escape from the awful freedom of your built-in loneliness is this sort of concoction, this pseudo-community of things and people with one another, each of which is really alone right down the line. The ethics of this procedure is also precarious. Here too you must act as if there are categorical imperatives making the demands of ordinary morality upon your conduct, but knowing all the time that these are without foundation and to be violated wherever necessary to the goal of coherent or well-ordered community. Thus you agree with Kant, realizing however that he was, like you, whistling in the dark, to give the whistler the illusion of not being alone.

The upshot of all this is that, first and last, there is your individual "existence" and the *Existenz* you give yourself by fiat in your subjective world; and, secondarily, the "objective" community you create precariously for yourself with others. ("Objective" here simply must have those shudder-quotes.)

This gets me to the main point about the new "political consciousness" in my century. If you are thinking existentially about this, like Sartre, you will be impressed with the need for another fiction, namely, that of the State with a Will of its own, embodied in the political leaders. Without this, no society of lonely individuals could ever be whipped into shape. The individual wills of Tom and Dick and Harry can't be expected to forge a coherent *society*. Only each its own subjective world. But since Will is the only force capable of creating order or community of any sort with the air of something essential about it, and since there is a body politic, there must be political leadership with the right and power of voluntary fiat to produce and regulate its socio-political unity. This cannot reasonably be expected to be genuine community because there is no such thing, really. It is political consciousness of collaborating in support of The Cause, as declared by The Leader, that cements things together into a society; not the sentimental spontaneity of friendly individuals. So democratic liberalism is false, and Sartre sympathises with Communism. (This summary statement is my way of putting the argument. Sartre's is much more involved.

Of course, the kind of reasoning that will show all this most persuasively is dialectical. There will have to be much subtle pitting of extreme opposites against one another—fiction versus fact, individual versus State, freedom versus political authority, ethical versus supra-ethical consciousness—with the air of finally reconciling them in dramatic syntheses. Only dialectical reason, in the Hegelian sense, can do that. So Sartre simply had in the end to make a sustained defense of dialectic. In 1960 the first part of an enormous work with that aim appeared, *Critique de la raison dialectique.*

25.

Now I am equipped to drive home my point about the relation between this new political consciousness and the new technology. Sartre tries, in his *Critique de la raison dialectIque*, to show that both his own existential thinking and Marx's dialectic are scientific, in a vein that reminds one of similar attempts of Communist thinkers. Now I can understand why one should be concerned to make a show of scientific thinking if he is doing, say, biology. The Russians got especially nervous when their thinking in genetics took an unscientific turn, as it did also in their physics under pressure of the demands of their dialectical materialism, against which some of their present physicists are openly revolting. Of course, this twist was required of it by the ideology. But why try so stridently to show that the ideology itself is scientific? If one wants to proceed in a manner that is scientifically questionable on the level of an empirical discipline like biology and physics, it would seem that the justification for this would be a doctrine that there are higher or supra-scientific disciplines that legislate over science, with the right to direct and even overrule it. The Metaphysical Chair rules that. . . etc. The Hegelian Dialectic was precisely this sort of book of parliamentary procedure, looking down upon the empirical sciences and issuing verdicts about The Truth, *ex cathedra*. And it was from this book in dialectical ("constructive") phenomenology that the existentialists and the Marxists got their lessons. Why then do they want to make the dialectically formulated ideology itself look scientific instead of metaphysical?

The answer takes shape in view of the notion of creation of objects by objectification. In the earlier German dialectical idealism, from Fichte to Hegel, the picture was of an Absolute Spirit creating for itself an environing world of objects by self-objectifications. This productive operation was a demonstration of the absolute power of Spirit to confer existence, meaning and value on objects, by ordering them in satisfaction of its own inner demands that were concealed from the finite intelligences included in the inferior realm of created objects. The Absolute was supposed to realize itself in such manifestations of itself to itself, *via* these creations, but those German metaphysicians also insisted that there was always a residue of Pure Spirit left unrealized in any single stage of self-objectification. So it could make further demands, as ruthless and unethical as need be, to the established moral order of the given society of objects in its sphere of influence. My account of this traditional German idealism is a faithful reflection especially of Hegel's philosophy of the evolution of human society.

Now it makes all the difference in the world how this self-objectifying Spirit is conceived. For Sartre, it is broken down into the plurality of miserable human selves that project each its own little world of objects and that themselves are objects to one another. Just objects. This leaves society pretty disintegrated, calling for the superior fiat of a Collective Will that galvanises it for collective action, treating the member selves deliberately as objects or instruments for its purpose and requiring them even to treat one another, not as persons and as ends in themselves, but as objects and as mere means to the realization of the Collectivizing Agency. Not that Sartre thinks that this is good. He is explicit about the evil condition of humanity, and is dramatically sorry that there is no God, and that Kant was so wrong in his doctrine of ultimate ethical requirements. In his *Saint Genet* he regretfully adopts rules of procedure that are the antithesis of Kant's ethics of categorical imperatives. The rules we must actually live by require us to violate these, by treating one another as objects and as means to the Cause of as much social togetherness as is permitted mankind. Thus are anguish and guilt built into taking social action. There is no society possible without such evil conduct, and the only feasible ethics is the "ethics of ambiguity"—the title of Simone de Beauvoir's book.

The natural panacea or complement for such a view is Communism. It seems tailored for the job. It provides the otherwise missing optimism and confidence for collective action, while agreeing that God and ultimate ethical requirements are out of order. It exudes and indoctrinates the *dogmatic* commitment to the Cause and to the unethical conduct necessary to its fulfillment. Existentialism by itself cannot provide this. But insisting on the importance of practical and theoretical *engagement* as much as it does, it simply cries out to be supplemented by Communism. So whatever complexion existentialism is to have as social and political message, it will get it from Marxism. Better yet, Leninism. The complexion is ruddy, a cross between red and pink. Beneath this and concealed by it is the blue pallor of the sickness onto death that Kierkegaard made into a condition of becoming religious. One might say that Communism is the scab hardening over the suppurating sore of existentialism beneath with the appearance of healing. Perhaps the real cure would come with a fuller recognition of the demands that religion and ethics make on interpersonal relations, but this is a moot point; moreover, it is precisely such recognition that the ethos of my century is making more and more difficult if not impossible, thanks to the Spirit of Technology as the new Absolute and its massive automation.

As Communism provides the doctrine that confirms and justifies the socio-political tendencies in both camps, so does the spirit of the new technology at present determine this Communist doctrine. According to the explicit doctrine, the modes of economic production are the basic determinant. But these themselves are being powerfully determined by the terrific eruption of technological intelligence in my century. Technological determinism, not economic, is emerging as the final philosophy. This, in effect, is how the "self-objectifying Spirit" is now being conceived. The objects that it creates out of itself are not only television, radar, and nuclear reactors but also the people who use them. All are its objects and instruments — instruments for the use of instruments. First- and second-order instruments, if you like, but all instruments nevertheless to the end of technological display. This is how the new Spirit manifests itself and its power. And the show has only begun, though it is already a frightfully fine one. Computers now are in the forefront of it. The political "consciousness" that Lenin prescribed, while proscribing "spontaneity" as bourgeois, has turned out to be the expression of this sort of Absolute Spirit, all else being the objects of its self-objectifications. Emptying the individual human self to make room for the occupation and domination of this Ultimate is now conceived as our final obligation and as the only road to social salvation. This, at bottom, is what it now is to be politically conscious, plus respect for the leaders of the transnational Party as the mouth-piece of the new Spirit and as the managers of men everywhere. And this new political consciousness is potentially as ubiquitous as science itself, and as impersonal.

This Spirit is subtly contagious now even in technologically backward countries. Their politically conscious leaders tend to demand aid first in the form of advanced electronic and nuclear devices as a symbol of their affiliation with the brave new world, with food, clothes, shelter, and general education coming second, though these be the greater natural need among their simple people. The insistence of this demand perplexes some of the donor-nations with foreign aid programs not for robots but for human beings.

Even where the demand is not directly for "progress" in this technological direction but for some other more humane commodity such as better education in the humanities, the model for improvement is still technology. I am thinking of the small colleges in my country that have been denied support by big Foundations because they are too slow to hold up the norm of experimental progress in industry as their standard of perfection or self-realization, or to use broadcasting devices that minimize the personal relation between teacher and student.

26.

Some lonely voices have in my century protested such objectifications of everything, even people. Notably Berdyaev, as in his *The Beginning and the End*, written during the last World War. He complains that there are already too many politically conscious leaders with a mania for organizing the masses towards world unity, so he excludes himself from the pack for another and opposite kind of job. Unfortunately, this turns out to be the *extreme* opposite. He is against any and all objectifications and their objects. He is for a final subjectification of everything. This, for him, means bringing them back to, and dissolving them in, their source in Spirit. In short, ultimate reality for him is Subjective Spirit, in the swim of which he chooses to live, move and have his being as subject instead of object. This is a pure subjective idealism and therefore—as Bosanquet would say—a false idealism. A true idealism does not conceive the material things of Nature as a degradation of Mind or Spirit by objectification, or as a fall from Grace. Mind and Matter supplement one another in an organic relation, the one requiring the other for its realization in reciprocal dependence.

What I find wanting in Berdyaev's view is a proper notion of, and respect for, things and thinghood. He is right about there being something not final or ultimate about *objects*, as was Rilke. But, as Rilke remarked and I have argued before, objects are abstractions from *things*. Things appear as this or that sort of objects, according to the exclusive and special way they are experienced. In such exclusive or "objectifying" relations, one does not become intimate or personal with them. But one may love or befriend things *per se*, in a quite humane rapport with them. In such a relation, nature is a place in which the human spirit is at home. It is precisely this consciousness of things, including persons, that is disrupted by the new political consciousness with its strident reduction of everything to objects-for-use, a demand that minimizes the reality and value of persons and of personal relations to things.

Still, it would be a mistake to suppose that the sort of recognition that the communist ideology gives objects makes it scientific in temper. A science submits, in observation, to objects for confirmation. Not so an ideology in praise of the Spirit of Technology. It presents objects, including people, as creatures or creations of that sort of Intelligence. It is the objects—again, including people—that must do the submitting, under dictation. They are for use by that technological Intelligence, which rather orders them instead of observing and learning from them.

The kind of scepticism about *empirically* grounded beliefs that emerges out of this, and its contrast with a more Humean kind, is brought out in the following essay. Call it "Scepticism and Ideology." I feel myself shifting into professional gear for that bit of writing, so the style will be a bit formal.

27.

My point is about the scepticism or the ideology that has become systematic in a theory. It does not concern the tid-bit sceptical or ideological beliefs that occasionally move any man. In short, I am discussing the sort of scepticism that, say, Hume inflated into a philosophy, and the sort of ideology that, say, the communists have also philosophically elaborated under the Marx-Lenin banner. And my argument is that such scepticism and ideology are fundamentally alike. They are in the same philosophical boat, where they will float or sink together, by the same logic.

It will take a bit of logico-psycho-analysis to show this, but nothing very involved. The basic concurrence or agreement of the two schools of thought is around the notion of object and of objectivity. Both camps are prone to undercut these concepts and give them cavalier treatment. This is their fundamental accord. Moreover, both were prompted to their scepticism of the Object and Objectivity by the transcendentalism of the new metaphysics under the influence of science. According to this metaphysics, the objects both of ordinary experience-and-belief and of religious experience-and-belief are transcendent and thus beyond the pale of knowledge. They are unknowable X's or, if cognitive access to them is to be had, it is quite circuitous involving faith or a curious guess-work. Scepticism follows as a kind of enlightenment, an emancipation from superstitions.

If the cast of mind is initially and primarily scientific, the emancipation will be from the ordinary beliefs of common sense about perception, its objects and the merely apparent objectivity of the relations that seem to order them into a cosmos. This is the scepticism usually called "philosophical." If the cast of mind is at first primarily religious or "existential" and practical, the enlightenment will claim to free people from ordinary beliefs about the objects and objectivity of traditional institutions, such as church and state, while providing for collective action by postulating "objectives." Such scepticism is ideological. Instead of an appeal to objects and objectivity, the appeal is to objectives-to-be-attained through the will to believe in them, and these serve as the organizers for concerted action in lieu of the traditional principles of authority with their antecedently real objects. Along with this goes, of course, an attitude of contempt for the objects and objectivity of scientifically controlled observation as a control on the fundamental beliefs.

Philosophical scepticism such as Hume's will continue to favor theoretical science for its own sake, while philosophically aware of its lack of a rational foundation and justification. Its maxim is: seek the detachment of scientific clarity and objectivity—and distrust it as a philosopher. The ideological sceptic such as Lenin favors the development of science only as a practical discipline, in technological applications that implement the power of the collective drive toward objectives postulated by the ideology.

In other words, the philosophical sceptic (Hume) continues to toy with the notions of objectivity and object, in a kind of as-if stance which he considers necessary to as much sanity as possible for a man. When he takes to action, he acts as if there are those objects and their laws though, as a philosopher, he knows that these transcend experience and knowledge. In such action, he is motivated by a simple "animal faith" which he smiles upon as a philosopher. Not so with the ideological sceptic, whose cast of mind was originally religious and remains that way after the rejection of the Object of theology. Collective action with its postulated objectives is the ultimate for him. When he participates in such action, he has no smiles for anything, not even for theoretical science as the contemplative rapport with objects that it is alleged to be. He frowns on it. To toy with it is to toy with infidelity. His maxim is: seek the dynamic obscurity of ideologically motivated thought-in-action—and trust it. There is nothing better or even possible for a man. Sanity for him depends on his realizing this, according to the communist. Or if sanity is the wrong word for this, call it salvation, which after all is the important thing from the ideological point of view. The ideological consciousness is thoroughly redemptive, so there is something demonic about it in its sense of what people must be saved from and of the sometimes killing discipline they must be subjected to. Sanity, alongside this state of mind, then looks trivial in its contemplative detachment from the deeply involved concerns of mankind. It is for the birds and the bourgeoisie. A sort of secular puritanism is built into this ideological mentality, as fierce as the theological sort. It makes a principle, for example, of not producing world champions in such pleasant and gentlemanly sports as golf.

Both the philosophical and the ideological scepticisms of objects and objectivity will pose as if their positions, though different in the above respects, follow from a proper understanding of science. More than that, each will claim to be "truly scientific" in some sense. The Marxist, having gotten rid of The Object of theology, simply bulges with the sense of his enlightened scientific secularism, while pulsating with a savior's love of Humanity. As a dialectical materialist, he is forced to *claim* he is an objectivist concerned with real objects. He presents himself as the only reliable philosopher of religion, whose primary function is a debunking one in relation to its *traditional* objects. Diagnosis of his position shows that his concern is really with *objectives* or goals of passionate action. The Humean, having dissolved away the objects and beliefs of common sense in the acid of the true understanding of the subjective ground of science, takes on the airs of the only reliable philosopher of science, while sympathizing with mankind over the precariousness of human knowledge.

It is as if science has redeemed both of them, by their seeing through it to its non-scientific foundations. The philosophical sceptic like Hume or Santayana would thereafter save men by the gentle force of disillusionment, and the ensuing detachment and dispassionateness. The ideological sceptic like Lenin prepares to save men from The Object of religion and its institutions by the demonic force of absolute attachment or commitment to the objectives of the ideology, transferring the original theological passion to The Cause of the Party, without any diminution of passionateness. He simply replaces the priestly hierarchy with the political. Thus does the Humean retain his original scientific cast of mind, and the communist the disposition that was initially practical and religious; while both operate under the influence of the scientific ethos and so make claims to Enlightenment. The metaphysics of this perspective jeopardizes objects and objectivity in both camps.

The religious quality of the communist's response is evidenced by the favor that theologians confer upon it, in preference to philosophical scepticism of the Humean sort. The arch-examples are among the existentialists in theology, such as Tillich. So impressed has Tillich been with the religious cast of mind of communism that he has condoned even its atheism—the jettisoning of The Object of religious experience. But, as a dialectical theologian, he of course criticizes the Marxist *complete* rejection of the notion of transcendence. God, as the ground of being, transcends everything, but without eliminating His immanence. The solution is thus paradoxical, as is the language of religion.

The scientific disposition undergirding the Humean sceptic's position is attested by the honorable mention most philosophers of science give him, despite the demurrers that sometimes accompany the praise, as a corrective for his radical scepticism of objects. In *some* sense, they say, there are objects to which we have cognitive access, though Hume's scepticism was justified in relation to the Cartesian notion of the transcendent "external world." Such qualified praise parallels the sort which the existential theologians give communist ideology in relation to the religious Object, toning down the wholesale scepticism by giving it a dialectical twist.

The people who are fond of Hume will dislike this juxtaposition of philosophical scepticism with communist ideology, calling it a device for conferring guilt by association. And the ideologically inclined people will dislike it for the same reason, seeing Hume as a menace to their faith. So it will be interesting to go on to an evaluation. The spirit of the exposition so far has been quite neutral. But now we ask, which position is more reasonable?

We might profitably begin with the consideration of the general question: what breeds any scepticism of the wholesale or comprehensive theoretical sort we have in view? This is different from the question as to what makes or made people sceptical about this or that particular issue. The question is: what makes anyone sceptical wholesale about knowledge-claims, either in general, or in science (mystics), or in religion (scienticism), or in art (several -isms here), or in evaluational discourse including ethics (positivism), etc.? Is it something built into the nature of things and the human condition relative to them? To be progressively discovered by more and more enlightened insights? (Notice right here that anyone who answers this affirmatively is committed willy-nilly to some ideal of objectivity of judgment. Even after an appeal to Russell's theory of types.)

Let us lean on some historical examples for a suggestion of the answer. Locke's scepticism of the knowledge of the *essence* of material substance, what generated it? The main influence was

Descartes' conception of it. And Berkeley's scepticism of the *existence* of material substance? It was mainly Locke's negative conception of what material things essentially are. And Hume's scepticism of knowledge of the external world? Berkeley's conception of material things as clusters of sensations? And Kant's scepticism of knowledge of things-in-themselves? What Hume did to the concept of them. And Hegel's scepticism of anything outside Absolute Mind? Kant's sort of scepticism. And Kierkegaard's scepticism of Hegel's rationalism? What Hegel called rational or what he made of the concept of reason. And the logical positivist's scepticism of evaluations as having any cognitive force? The reaction of scientism both to Hegelian idealism and existentialism. Etc. One is reminded of Moore's remark that a philosopher addresses his thinking to his predecessors, or contemporaries, in philosophy.

But it would be a caricature to suppose that there were no other influences, nothing else in view, in the above cases. Any great philosopher has in view also the nature of things and the human condition, though he tends to look at them through the lenses of the established language of philosophy with its tap-root in the great tradition. He is subject, moreover, to other influences in the ethos of his time, like any human being.

Still, surveying the history of theoretical scepticism, one naturally gets the impression that a good deal of it was generated not so much by the nature of things and of the human condition *per se* as by perplexing concepts of these. This impression has been growing in strength especially among philosophers themselves, who used to be the famous sceptics. Now it is they who smile wisely at the scepticism sparking the ideological commitment to the juggernauts of collective action on the one hand, and at the wraiths of philosophical scepticism on the other. Their maxim now is: in deciding what is the case, *look* before you think and speak. Of course, they recognize the complication in this effort to break out through the heritage of preconceptions into a conceptually innocent looking which is supposed to control philosophical thinking. They do not forget that thinking and language give the looking itself its point and its intelligence; looking, thinking, and speaking go together in relations of reciprocal influence.

If this complex sort of thing is the case, and the look-before-you-think maxim is abided by in deciding it, "looking" here will be a higher-order, phenomenological awareness or consciousness of the various categorically different ways of experiencing things, and of the different logic of the expression of each. This too is the case, and it is fundamentally this which present-day philosophers are becoming acute about, with a new neutrality or non-partisanship about the special modes.

In the continental camp that used to be just ideological (with Hegel's blessing), this consciousness has developed through and beyond existentialism to phenomenology— *vide* Merleau-Ponty—which at present is reminding us of what might be called post-metaphysical presuppositions. "Post" is better here than "pre-" because the neutrality with respect to this or that theory is *thoughtfully* arrived at and purchased. It is the fruit of conceptual discipline and enlightenment. As one phenomenologist puts it, what the phenomenologists are now doing is metaphysics-beyond-metaphysics. (The continental European philosopher still likes paradoxes, but with much of the poison taken out.)

In the Anglo-American camp, where Humean philosophical scepticism used to be at home, the new phenomenological consciousness is also at work, though with more attention to logic and language than to modes of perception which is the meat of the continentals. But "ways of looking" is now a common expression even among the Anglo-American analysts. So, in this case, one man's meat has ceased to be another man's poison. The difference is a matter of emphasis, though at first glance it looks like an unlikely meeting of extremes. Even among the analysts one now hears talk about "descriptive" metaphysics (Strawson) and the "phenomenology of language" (Austin).

This is their way of doing metaphysics-beyond-metaphysics. The contrast is with the older partisan tendency to do "constructive" metaphysics with the old aggressiveness and partisanship if ideological, or sick with the pale cast of dispassionate thought if philosophically sceptical. (Hume too was an old-style metaphysician.) The presiding genius over the new Anglo-American performance is the later Wittgenstein who, in his own tortured way, put on a persuasive exhibit of doing philosophy-beyond-philosophy, and its incalculable importance for human sanity.

The question about such an ideology as communism on the one hand and philosophical scepticism on the other, which is more reasonable? is finally in a frame-work that suggests the right answer.

People can be persuaded wholesale to attachments or detachments. A "wholesale" persuasion involves bad reasoning. It does this naturally because it is motivated by a concept of reason which is not warranted either by the nature of things or human nature—a concept which is spawned by an unwarranted favoring of subjects and subjectivity at the expense of objects and objectivity. This partisanship at the level of theory is what generates the subordinate ones. (This theoretical bias has been countered in the history of philosophy by an equally artificial and unfortunate partisan stand in favor of objects and objectivity, which is not treated in this essay.) The result is an insufficiently controlled attachment to, or the same sort of detachment from, something "in general." The consequence of this is mutilation in some form or other.

The ideological sort of scepticism of objects and objectivity is responsible for attachments that mutilate by uncontrolled positiveness. Philosophical scepticism is guilty of the negative mutilation of detachment. Which is more reasonable? They score a tie on that count, as failures. But the former does seem more dangerous than the other, as long as the latter makes room for the animal faith necessary to the simple, uncollectivized actions necessary to survival.

28.

A very sensitive protest to the massive technologizing that is going on is found in Gabriel Marcel's little book *The Existential Background of Human Dignity*. The argument is less dogmatic and metaphysical than Berdyaev's. It is more dramatically persuasive—Marcel has written many plays—and more apprehensive over the fate of the individual person caught in the political and economic machinery of my century, thanks to advances of technology. Karl Jaspers also has similar fears, warning us of the tendency in our time of the "people" to evolve into the "public," and the "public" into the "masses," despite the strident affirmation of political leaders that their aim is to establish a "people's" or a "democratic" republic. The consummation of such an evolution would be a herd of organisms, not a community of persons or individuals. And they would be regimented, each as a means to a Collective Cause, by managers. Our two existentialist philosophers above refuse to collaborate in such a scheme, either as members of the common herd or as its managers. I like to call what they so wisely are avoiding the "political consciousness," which measures the value of a man solely in relation to the degree of his collective collaboration.

29.

Both these scepticisms of objects-and-objectivity, the philosophical and the ideological, tend to leave human action too unrestricted by principles of right conduct. They put it beyond ethics. They give it license to move rapidly and ruthlessly toward the realization of wants, of the individual if the scepticism is Humean, of the Party if it is Leninist. Using people as mere means *en route* wherever convenient. The individualist, like Hume, will of course be content usually to act under ethical restrictions, by convention and for comfortable pragmatic reasons. The collectivist, like Lenin, will fiercely demand the ethical violations of individual rights, on the principle that The Cause requires it.

It has occurred to a group of thinkers called the New Conservatives that the way to stem this tide is to argue the importance of the institutions that are crumbling in its current. I am thinking of Russell Kirk and his *The Conservative Mind* (1953), which is the bible of the New Conservatism. This sort of thinking gets its nurture from *Reflections on the Revolution in France* by Edmund Burke. The outlook here is comparable to Toynbee's in history (in his middle period) and to Eliot's in literature. Eliot is known to have said that he is an Anglo-Catholic in religion, a royalist in politics, and a classicist in literature. But the last two sentences are taken from an essay of mine titled "Beyond Ethics?" that I was asked to do as a survey of recent developments in ethics and ethical consciousness for the East-West Philosophers' Conference in Hawaii. It is published in *Philosophy and Culture – East and West* [1962]. Since it provides a context for things I want to say subsequently, I present it in full next. It includes the rest of the account of the New Conservatism mentioned above. The style is academic or professional.

30.

A. Beyond Being

Plato, after having described essence as Being at its best or as pure Being, made a remark that set the stage for centuries of subsequent metaphysics, ethics, and theory of value. He said that "the good . . . far exceeds essence in dignity and power."[1] On the whole, the mighty opposites that, until the turn of our own century, issued from this distinction between Being and something beyond Being can be put under two very general heads, naturalism and super-naturalism.

In this opposition, the naturalists tended to identify "what is" or Being with Nature, and to take arms against the notion of *anything* else. Even ideals and values—the good—were assigned a derivative and dependent natural status in the realm of essential Being. Essence comes first and determines everything, was the slogan of these naturalists. Beginning with the seventeenth century, in the flush of the scientific era, naturalism portrayed essence or

---

[1] B. Jowett, trans., *The Republic* (New York: Modern Library, Inc., 1941), p. 250.

Being as consisting of "primary qualities," those most congenial to the mathematical conception of the exact natural sciences. Beyond such Being there are only the secondary and tertiary qualities of sensation and valuation, which were thought of at subjective and only "in the mind." Remember Descartes and Galileo and Locke.

The supernaturalists reacted to this with a vengeance, but on the basis of a surprising agreement with the naturalists. They agreed on the conception of Nature as primarily the domain of the objects of scientific observation and understanding, and that the rest is indeed "in the mind." But what a mind! Metaphysical and objective idealism emerged to declare that Absolute Mind or Spirit is the comprehensive ground of the Being of everything, including Nature, transcending it and far exceeding it in dignity and power. Thus was Plato's good reinstated with a vengeance, as something beyond and better than *natural* essence or Being. The ought-to-be, the ideal (with ontological import), took precedence over what is. Kant's cautious and critical statement of this position is perhaps the best, less embarrassed with confusions than the heavy post-Kantian development culminating in Hegel.

This is an old story which the West knows and loves, and it reminds one of the similar wonderful Eastern story of the plunge from Being into Non-Being. But my concern and my present duty are to pass on to another story of the twentieth century which is not so generally well known—or loved. The nerve of the old or classical story of opposition had to do with the conflict between Being and something better than Being. Up to the turn of our century, the philosophical theses and antitheses made it look as if there were a cosmic conflict—or at least a distinction—between Being and the Good, *where even the Good is construed as an extraordinary kind or way of Being—a something* that is better than ordinary, natural existence. The Oriental story, with its beautiful and expressive paradoxes, about Non-Being approached via *neti-neti* renunciation also confirms this remark. This whole issue takes on another complexion in the twentieth century, to the account of which I now anxiously turn. We must first patiently refresh our memories of twentieth-century developments in ethics and value-theory in the West, noticing especially what has happened in that area since our last conference of a decade ago. Then I shall be equipped to deal with the main issue, the question of whether philosophy is taking us "beyond ethics."

B. Conspectus of Recent Western Developments in Moral Thought

For Anglo-American philosophers, G. E. Moore is the Plato of the twentieth century, on the following count. In his *Principia Ethica*, of 1903, we find a proposition comparable to Plato's quoted above; and mighty opposites have issued from it since then, the polar opposition being similar in form to the classical, but very different in content. We must first get a bird's-eye view of this in its inception.

Moore's proposition, declared at the beginning of the century, is that good is a non-natural quality.[2] This sounds like Plato and the modern metaphysical idealists, but let us look cautiously at Moore's meaning. In the first place, he does *not* mean that something called "good" is better than natural qualities, such as pleasant, intelligent, or even cool and sweet and bright blue. Though he calls good a non-natural quality, his main concern is *not* to assert the extraordinary being of something that far exceeds natural qualities in dignity and power. His

---

[2] G. E. Moore, *Principia Ethica* (Cambridge: University Press, 1903), chap. I.

point is a logical one, not an ontological. He is analyzing the meaning of any expression of the form "*x* is good," where *x* is any natural quality, thing, or state of affairs. He has noticed that one can significantly ask of *anything* natural, "Is it good?" and this to him is evidence that good cannot itself be simply identified with, or defined as, anything natural. So, he persists in taking good as a simple, unanalyzable, non-natural quality, which may or may not qualify anything in Nature. He is distinguishing the predicate "good," as of a different logical type, from any "natural" predicate, such as those listed above. To suppose that it is not this sort of non-natural predicate, and to identify it with some natural quality, such as pleasant, or object-of-interest, are to commit the "naturalistic fallacy." All philosophers who define "good" in this way—indeed, who attempt to define or analyze it in *any* way—commit this fallacy. Good is good, and that is that. Anything may be qualified by this non-natural quality, but must not be identified with it. (What it qualifies may *also* be pleasant or desired, etc., and these things will be "the goods" of life.) Moore is saying in effect that the adjective "good" has a peculiar meaning inasmuch as it does not name (stand for, refer to) any natural quality. But it *does*, he asserts, name a non-natural quality—something beyond the being of anything natural.

Such a position is apparently pregnant with a new and vexing sort of Platonism. It soon generated critical questions. How is *this* distinction between natural and non-natural to be interpreted, with its veiled logical instead of ontological concern? Is the question still the old one, about *what* "good" means and the nature of this element, or is it not now in effect a new question, namely, *how* this value-predicate and others mean? Are value-terms descriptive predicates, such as "pleasant" and "cool"? In short, are they to be treated as "cognitively" significant terms, in expressions that are true (or false) of "values"?

A great division formed around this issue, but this time it was not the old naturalism vs. supernaturalism; it was naturalism vs. non-naturalism, where *both* of these opposites were primarily concerned with the logic of valuation—the question of *how* value-expressions signify or under what controls. And so, the period of "meta-ethics" began. The new naturalists in ethics and theory of value argued that the logic of moral judgment and valuation is identical with that of the factual, natural sciences. And, to set the stage for this demonstration, they rejected Moore's notion of good as a non-natural quality intuitively prehended. The presence of such a quality would spoil the performance of ordinary empirical method, which depends on controlled observations and predictions. Values can be known, according to the twentieth-century naturalists. This means that knowledge-claims can appropriately be made in this connection; and this involved holding that "x is good" is of the same logical type as "x is edible," where both "edible" and "good" are "constructs" of the sort that are under the nice cognitive controls operative in the empirical sciences.

Before mentioning some of these naturalists, and the opposing non-naturalists, let us remember that this growing logic-and-language consciousness was not confined to philosophy. The scientists had also been jarred into this new method-consciousness by developments in physics—Einstein's special and general theories of relativity in 1905 and 1915. These, together with the strange quantum mechanics, made the scientists also wonder about *how* the language of science signifies instead of just *what* it means. The same phenomenon appeared in art, with the new formalism of abstractionism. Art analysts became obsessed with the question of how a work of art means—poem, painting, or musical composition. It is as if another stage of the self-conscious had been reached, where the "self" seemed to be man as a symbolizing animal, to use Cassirer's phrase.

But, back to the new naturalists. R. B. Perry,[3] influenced by behavioral psychology with its concern to bring psychological statements under observational controls, defined value as the object of any interest, construing interest non-intrespectively. He hoped thus not only to make "good" observable but especially to make value-judgments confirmable. A valuation makes cognitive sense, under the established logic of factual inquiry. Notice that the primary concern here is not pointedly to say what value is as a quality of an object. The aim is, rather, to give an analysis of valuations which will subject them to standard confirmation, as is the question of what good "essentially" is had been outmoded.

The same motive is conspicuous in John Dewey's treatment. He argues that good is a "construction,"[4] meaning to make a methodological

---

[3] *General Theory of Value* (New York: Longmans, Green & Co., 1926).
[4] *The Quest for Certainty* (New York: Milton Balch & Co., 1929).

point rather than an ontological one. This is why this sort of naturalism is ontologically so accommodating—it leaves *that* question open. He is anxious lest moral judgments and value-judgments be exempted from the control of the ordinary logic of inquiry and decision. He notices how we cannot be said to know anything until we form a construct or concept of it which connects it with conditions of its occurrence and permits its stabilization or production at will. This is the difference featured between "having" or simply experiencing a *desired* something, on the one hand, and knowing it under controls that define it as *desirable*, on the other, with a premium being placed on the latter.

Similar remarks apply to another prominent naturalist in value-theory, C. I. Lewis.[5] The "expressive statements" which simply announce the presence of a "had" or immediate quality (*quale*) of enjoyment are not value-judgments. They make no claims to knowledge: they do not make cognitive sense. (Note what happens, on this ground, to Moore's expression of a simply intuited quality of good.) Only when value is *construed* as an objective property of something does it become knowable,

---

[5] *Analysis of Knowledge and Valuation* (Chicago: Open Court Publishing Co., 1946), especially pp. 373-396.

and it is then expressed in "non-terminating judgments," which formulate definite expectations of various consequences of the knowledge-claim, and these either confirm the judgment or upset it—as in the case of any factual ascription of any property. Lewis goes further than Dewey in making it explicit that he is deliberately ambiguous about the description of value as a quality. He calls it vaguely a "dimension-like mode or quality, something like enjoyment but not to be exclusively identified with this. It is worth noticing, finally, that Lewis, unlike Dewey, distinguishes such *valuations* from *ethical* imperatives of a more Kantian sort. These, he acknowledges significantly, are *not* empirical statements, subject to cumulative experiential testing. With this distinction I shall be much concerned later, in a more general context.

These samples suffice to show that the new school of thought is appropriately called "logical naturalism," to distinguish it from the earlier metaphysical or ontological variety. I turn now to an account of its opposition, calling it "logical non-naturalism" in ethics and theory of value.

The first conspicuous (and notorious) version of this is the logical positivists', with which I shall not stay long, since it is so well known the world over. It emerged in the twenties of our century. R. Carnap and A. J. Ayer, operating under the spell of the language of physics as the paradigm, accept Moore's pronouncement that "good" (in fact, any value-term) does not denote any natural quality. But, they add that it is not used to describe or name *any* quality. Its meaning is not descriptive at all. One misinterprets its sense if he thinks it functions as an adjective of factual assertion. Such a mistake tempts one to look for a quality called "goodness" in things or in the subjective response—e.g., pleasure—of people, and the search never succeeds. This is because value-terms and ethical terms signify in a different mode or way from terms in true or false statements. They signify expressively exactly as smiles or frowns do. Their meaning is thus "emotive," and value-judgments are pseudo-statements. According to the non-naturalists, the supposition that these are confirmable propositions is the mistake of the logical naturalists, who are still haunted by the ghost of the traditional assumption that valuations are true or false by reference to something or other.[6] This concept of emotive meaning of valuations was occasionally extended to include a "motivational" or imperative dimension,

---

[6] A. J. Ayer, *Language, Truth and Logic* (London: Gollanz, Ltd., 1936); R. Carnap, *Philosophy and Logical Syntax* (London: K. Paul, Trench, Trübner Co., Ltd., 1935).

making them something like grammatically veiled commands or requests. Thus, "This is wrong" would mean "Don't do this," on this interpretation.

The bible of emotivism is C. L. Stevenson's *Ethics and Language*.[7] Stevenson was motivated more by models in psychology than in physics, under the influence of Ogden and Richard's *Meaning of Meaning*.[8] Though this analysis of any expression of the form "x is good" resolves it into two components, "I approve of x; do so as well"—one a factual statement, the other an imperative—yet Stevenson is an astute enough psychologist to know that this complex expression lacks the *emotive* force of the simpler "x is good," since "good" is a dynamic term that kindles favorable feelings and attitudes, and triggers action. The concept of conditioned response is prominent here. Value-terms evoke feelings and modify attitudes, without the necessary intervention of ideas, though these may incidentally intervene in the process of emotive communication. Stevenson's method of "persuasive definition" is not as well known in this context as it should be. It is in some respects his most sensitive contribution. Value-

---

[7] New Haven: Yale University Press, 1944.

[8] C. R. Ogden and J. A. Richards (New York: Harcourt, Brace & Co., Inc., 1923).

terms may be "persuasively" defined. Given a sufficiently vague term with emotive (valuational) meaning, such as "cultured," it may be connected with other terms having descriptive or cognitive meaning, such as "intelligent," "erudite," "imaginative," etc., in a persuasive definition. The effect will be to evoke a favorable response to people having such characteristics, since to be "cultured" is already granted as "good." "Cultured" means emotively, as does "good," and thus tends to confer favor on anything to which it is applied. This is the way all value-terms mean; and *how* they mean is the main question, not *what* they mean. It will be seen that defining value-terms this way certainly does not get at, or expose, the "essence" of anything for what this meant in the classical tradition. And let us remember again that it was Moore's suggestion that "good" is an indefinable, non-natural quality which was bearing this kind of meta-ethical fruit, with the spotlight of attention turned on questions of *how* expressions mean.[9]

Our story of recent positivism, also called logical empiricism, ends with a brief mention of another psychologically oriented member of the

---

[9] Moore's concessions to Stevenson are startling: see his reply in P. Schlipp, ed., *The Philosophy of G. E. Moore* (Menasha, Wisconsin: Banta Publications Co., 1942).

movement, C. W. Morris.[10] For him, signs or expressions signify in (at least) three "modes of signifying": designative, appraisive, and prescriptive. Valuational expressions are interpreted as signifying mainly in the two latter. What distinguishes this account from the others in this group is Morris' attempt to fix a sense of "true" which allows even appraisals and prescriptions to be capable of truth or falsity—though they do not make designative or descriptive sense. The treatment is in the framework of behavioral psychology. But the significant thing in this connection is the first sign of a breakdown of the sharp positivistic distinction between the cognitive and non-cognitive functions of language, with respect to valuational discourse. Morris' theory is also significant for its classification of "types of discourse"—metaphysical, religious, poetic, scientific—which gives it a cosmopolitan complexion, an interest which was revealed earlier in his *Paths of Life*,[11] well known to many Eastern philosophers.

The deck has been cleared for the presentation of the remaining branch of this tree of logical non-naturalism, another development whose growth has

---

[10] *Signs, Language, and Behavior* (New York: Prentice-Hall, Inc., 1946).

[11] C. W. Morris, *The Paths of Life* (New York: Harper & Brothers, 1942).

by now all but hidden the positivistic ramification under its foliage, and whose contributions to *moral* philosophy have been made only in the last decade, since our last East-West conference. It is a much more subtle approach to our problems, with suggestions that do greater justice to the multifarious spirit of man as a language-using agent. This development is, on the whole, much less understood, especially in the East, than the logical positivism it is superseding with éclat. In fact, critics commonly make the mistake of supposing that these new "Oxford philosophers"—conveniently called this for short—are still positivists, while what actually defines the new approach is its rejection of the logical-positivistic verification theory of meaning together with the earlier logical atomism and the tendency to hold scientific method up as the model for all serious discourse. The genius of the new philosophy is the *later* Wittgenstein, expressed at first in the nineteen-thirties in the *Blue and Brown Books*[12] (published later in 1958) and in *Philosophical Investigations* (1953).[13] The chief and the best points are made in the form of mercurial aphorisms or enigmatic suggestions which tax the imagination. We turn now to a short survey of this new current, which in the area of ethics is only a

---

[12] Oxford: B. Blackwell, 1958.

[13] Oxford: B. Blackwell, 1953.

decade old, and which by all odds is the most conspicuous development in the Anglo-American world and Scandinavia during the decade.

The keynote of the Oxford philosophy is that people do all sorts of things with their living language, and these various uses are the meanings. This highlights the concept of "performatory meaning," a good first approximation to which we get in Margaret Macdonald's treatment.[14] Here the outlook is partly anthropological, like that of Malinowski in his studies of the primitive uses of language; so, the model of ritualistic performance or expression looms large, as the standard of interpretation for ethical utterance.

Macdonald rejects emotivism in ethics as featuring too lyrical, subjective, or private a mode or expression. The model of true-false factual statement must be put aside, she agrees with the emotivists, as against Moore; to say "x is good" does not describe any quality of anything. But the affair of making moral judgments is too serious, fraught with public sanction, to be characterized as emotive. They must be treated "ceremonially" and invested "with an

---

[14] "Ethics and the Ceremonial Use of Language," in Max Black, ed., *Philosophical Analysis* (Ithaca: Cornell University Press, 1950).

authority to affect action.... Moral judgments are thus impersonal verdicts of a common moral ritual . . . they are the language of a rite in which we are all lifelong performers."[15] The analogy is with verdicts of guilty or not guilty formally uttered in a court of law. This, according to Macdonald, is *how* moral utterances mean—without making any (true-false) statement of "objective fact" or without describing any properties at all, natural or non-natural.

This theme of "performatory" meaning, fathered in the special Oxford way mainly by J. L. Austin,[16] is given a variation by H. L. A. Hart, who portrays moral discourse as having a sort of "ascriptive" sense. To say, "Fred *did* it," speaking morally, is in effect *not* simply a description or even report of an action, but the *ascription* of a responsibility, in relation to certain rights.[17] But the variation on this theme that has drawn most attention is the concept of "commendatory" meaning. To say "This is good" or "Slandering is wrong" is to perform the act of commending or

---

[15] *Ibid.*, p. 229.

[16] See his "Other Minds," in Anthony G. Flew, ed., *Essays in Logic and Language*, Second Series (New York: Philosophical Library, 1953).

[17] "The Ascription of Responsibility and Rights," in Anthony G. Flew, ed., *Essays in Logic and Language*. First Series (New York: Philosophical Library, 1951).

condemning something, not to describe or further characterize it. Such judgments serve to *guide* choice, and to encourage or deter actions. (They do not *goad* choice by psychological incitement, as the emotivists believe.) Reasons may be given supporting the judgments, and the reasons will generally be factual or descriptive statements about properties of things or actual social patterns of conduct. But these are not to be mistaken as "defining the meaning" of the moral judgments, since a commendation is never a (true-false) description. That value-terms have also a dimension of descriptive meaning, in addition to their primary commendatory sense, is suggested (with reservations) by R. M. Hare.[18] But the earmark of valuations is consistently held to what, in the main, is done with them, their job of commending. And this is their performatory meaning. Like C. I. Lewis, these thinkers also tend to distinguish value-terms ("good") from ethical ("right"), and both of these from duty terms ("ought")—the point I converge on later.

The more important considerations come up in connection with the question of "justification" of moral judgments in this context of the new

---

[18] *The Language of Morals* (Oxford: Clarendon Press, 1952).

philosophy of the language of morals and values. S. Toulmin's treatment[19] is a fair sample, culminating in a dramatic view of the logic of ultimate valuational "decisions"—a view shared by others in the movement, and one which makes it akin to other ethical philosophies on the European continent and in the Orient. I shall elaborate on this important fact later, central as it is to the concern of this, our third conference [1959].

According to Toulmin, elementary moral judgments (commending this or that) fall under a hierarchy of rules, appeal to which justifies the judgments. There are first (moving up) the general maxims or rules of thumb governing right conduct, such as that telling lies is wrong. If these maxims themselves come under fire or are challenged, they are justified in turn by checking on their power to "harmonize" the satisfactions of members of the society. Now, if the whole "way of life" of the society is questioned, with other forms of life in view, something besides *moral* reasoning must be appealed to and a "personal decision" made, influenced by supra-moral considerations of the alternative patterns or cultures. Such an examination may comprise persuasive presentations

---

[19] *The Place of Reason in Ethics* (Cambridge: University Press, 1950).

of the alternatives, as in a great novel that gives the reader the feel of the total situations, or the agent may actually install himself in them one after another—trying them out. Choice of a way of life will not, at this level, be simply an act of *moral* decision. It will involve a crucial commitment or plunge, beyond the guidance of moral reason and will. Hare sounds a similar note, making the individual's decision look even more detached from rational considerations. Toulmin says there are traces of the existentialist mood in Hare's account. Yet, these Oxford philosophers do not intend to favor relativism in moral matters.[20] It is as if reality or Being were a character that things have *only* in the articulate framework of a "form of life" and its language. Things are objectively what they are only in such a reference-frame.

This subtle concept of a "form of life" is Wittgenstein's[21] in his later, more influential, phase. He associates this closely with the logic of the language, and this reminds one of Cassirer and Whorf.[22] But Wittgenstein's followers are not

---

[20] Hare, *op. cit.*, p. 143. Toulmin, *op. cit.*, pp. 206-209.

[21] Ludwig Wittgenstein, *Philosophical Investigations* (Oxford: B. Blackwell, 1953), p. 88c.

[22] See Harry Hoyer, ed., *Language in Culture* (Chicago: University of Chicago Press, 1954).

underwriting that kind of metaphysical idealism. Their point about language as a form of life is related to Wittgenstein's theory of aspects.[23] This tremendously fruitful concept needs to be elaborated in something like a descriptive metaphysics, and there now seems to be some recognition of the need, even among the Wittgensteinians.[24] Austin, for example, is beginning to speak of the philosopher's subject as "phenomenology of language." But more of this theme later.

On the whole, this new Oxford movement is the liveliest and most promising in current Anglo-American ethical thought. One remembers Nowell-Smith's book *Ethics*[25] also in this connection (1954). Before passing on rapidly through some other strands in the texture of the present-day moral mentality of the West, toward my main concern about East-West comparisons and constructive suggestions, let me just mention some recent efforts among sympathisers with the Oxford approach to transcend the strict individualism of the "personal-

---

[23] *Op. cit.*, pp. 193-215.

[24] See P. F. Strawson, *Individuals* (London: Methuen, 1959); also V. C. Aldrich, "Chess Not Without the Queen," *Proceedings of the American Philosophical Association*, 1958 [Presidential Address].

[25] P. H. Nowell-Smith, Pelican Books (Baltimore: Penguin Books, Inc., 1954).

decision" idea just mentioned,[26] in favor of an intercultural principle governing these ultimate decisions, thus giving them a moral rationale, after all. Even some recent naturalists, who are not sympathisers but only begrudgingly give recognition to the new anti-descriptivists and admit that value-terms are not simply descriptive, are co-operating in this effort to find a common ground for decision by *all* moral agents.[27]

Having raised this issue of whether there is a critical stage at which the individual is thrown back on his own resources, making the act of personal decision appear to be one of creative option *in vacuo*, we are in a position to look beyond the Anglo-American scene to the European continent, at existentialism. Though this philosophy is waning, and something like a more analytical phenomenology (Husserl, Hartmann, Scheler) is being revived there, it is still sufficiently viable to demand notice. An existentialist, *ethics* would be an anomaly, since the focal point of *Existenz* thinking is a metaphysical one about Being vs. Non-Being.

---

[26] K. Baier, "The Point of View of Morality," *Australian Journal of Philosophy* (1954), 104-135; J. Rawls, "Outline of a Decision Procedure for Ethics," *Philosophical Review*, LX, No. 2 (April, 1951), 177-197.

[27] E.g., P. B. Rice, *On the Knowledge of Good and Evil* (New York: Random House, 1955).

This is just what Heidegger argues in justifying his failure to produce a specific ethics.

The lack of such special ethical concern is characteristic of German thought of the last decade or more. Heidegger's dialectical metaphysics of Being provides a nook for the phenomenon called "conscience," connecting it with authenticity, but leaves it little chance to *operate* in the arena of existential conflicts, since it contains no useful regulations for conduct. Authenticity is demanded, but with a view more to *being* something than *doing* anything. Jasper's moral philosophy is comparable. The suggestion is that, as long as one loves, he may do as he pleases. "Love" here has a religio-metaphysical ring: a submissive rapport with what transcends the whole human scene of action—God as a metaphysical Absolute. A high commitment to this Absolute will give an indirect, ambiguous, provisional direction for authentic people below who are trying to do their duty. The act of commitment itself is supra-rational; there is no *logic* of obligation to this process. (Compare this with Eastern pronouncements.)

One might say, in view of such recent utterances (and earlier Hegelian ones), that the

German consciousness is an a-moral one, or tends toward this. Remember also Nietzsche's *Beyond Good and Evil*.[28] And it is this spirit that has permeated much of the East, on the professional philosophical level. I think first of Nishida and Nishitani in Japan, as just two star examples. In the creative literature of our period—the last decade—there is dramatic evidence of this tendency of existentialism to put a red pencil through morality in its ethical dimension, as something to be superseded. And, again, I mention only one prime example: *The Mandarins,* by Simone de Beauvoir,[29] devoted propagator of the existentialist faith of Jean Paul Sartre, who is supposed to have long been working out a specific existentialist ethics but has not yet produced one. There the chief characters are portrayed as by-passing ethical constraints (under sad necessity, to be sure) in favor of liberation and progress, according to an "ethics of ambiguity." This is man's tragic circumstance. But this view has connections with communist ideology, whose position relative to ethics I shall come to later. Here, too, we are beyond ethics, with a vengeance. So much for what is being called "Situation Ethics."

---

[28] Helen Zimmern, trans. (New York: Boni and Liveright, Inc., 1917).

[29] Cleveland: World Publishing Company, 1956.

Akin to this outlook is something outside professional philosophy, the new Protestant theology of Paul Tillich, consideration of which gets us back to the American scene, without breaking ties with the European. It is difficult to pick out any book of his which is specifically on ethics. The one that comes closest to qualifying is perhaps his *The Courage to Be*,[30] and the very title shows that it is a metaphysical treatise on Being—with Non-Being threatening to get the better of it. Tillich's existentialism began by having some of the theological and generally religious color one would expect under the brush-strokes of a professed theologian, and some bearing on Christian morals. It has of late passed more openly over into the camp of straight metaphysics, and other theologians are at last finding this out, to their dismay. In a recent pronouncement,[31] Tillich professed a return to Essence or Being, as deserving more notice than the incipient nihilism of his previous existentialism had given it. This "essentialism" is a revival of the thought of Hegel in his earlier stage, before even *The Phenomenology of Mind*.[32] though with affinities to this. And what of ethical principles?

---

[30] New Haven: Yale University Press, 1952.

[31] Kenyon College Lecture, 1959.

[32] J. B. Baillie, trans., 2 vols. (London: S. Sonnenschein & Co., Ltd.; New York: The Macmillan Co., 1910).

Tillich's answer is, at bottom, the old one of dialectical idealism. You get beyond them.

Reinhold Niebuhr does much better as a Christian and religious moralist[33] than his protégé Tillich. Both share the notion that the language of religion is mythic in some true or important sense of "myth," but Niebuhr does not forget this when he gets down to doing Christian ethics and theology. He is not just a philosopher as Tillich is. Man is caught in the "historical situation and must tragically act, of necessity, at times, participating in evil with others. But over him arches the rainbow of a humanly impossible perfection, an ideal of the perfect life symbolized by Christ, functioning as a catalyst that activates as righteous a life as possible here below. Again, the idea of absolute transcendence.

The difficulty of achieving a genuine moral community of highly civilised individuals, and of disclosing its rationale if any, is also featured by the depth psychologists in the wake of Freud. Freud's own thinking on this issue is concentrated in his

---

[33] *An Interpretation of Christian Ethics* (New York: Harper & Brothers, 1935).

Massenpsychologie,[34] in which the idea of such a society is left tense with an inner conflict. On the one hand, he makes the ruler or ruling faction look like a hypnotist with sadistic impulses, subjecting the people to a tranced obedience whose masochism permits, even invites, it. One would think, then, that he favors democratic individualism, but not so. In such a State, individuals are lonely, lost, and insecure. So, they tend naturally to escape from freedom (Erich Fromm), into the over-all social control of the Super-Ego imaged in the ruler. Yet, though Freud distrusts democracy as the final condition of well-being for the society, he hates dictatorship and is groping for a concept of individualism of some sort—individualism without optimistic liberalism or the old idea of salvation-by-education-for-democracy associated with American pragmatism. This is the problem that now preoccupies social psychologists who apply the psychoanalytic techniques to whole societies or culture-patterns. For example, David Riesman[35] characterized the earlier or rugged individual as "inner-directed" and not intelligently coordinated with the social pattern except in the limited

---

[34] *Massenpsychologie und Ich-Analyse* (Wien: Internationale & Psychoanalytischer Verlag, 1921).

[35] *Individualism Reconsidered* (Glencoe, Ill.: Free Press, 1954), esp. chap. VI. See also, Herbert Marcuse, *Eros and Civilization* (Boston: Beacon Press, 1955) for a prospectus with a more Jungian flavor.

conditions of "open capitalism," which has been outgrown. Now, another pressure-group pattern has emerged in which individuals have no core of individuality left. They are "other-directed." There is something "compulsive" about the behavior of both of these kinds of individuals. Then there are individuals who are still striving toward "autonomy"—the "saving remnant." The autonomous individual does not compulsively follow others, nor does he operate under a compulsion to flout them as does the primitive rugged individual. But, if we ask Riesman for the formula of this intelligent form of individualism, he will give the reply of a man on the threshold of unfamiliar ground: "We know almost nothing about the factors that make for such positive results; it is easier to understand the sick than to understand why some stay well."[36] This uncertainty is characteristic of others in the same camp, as is the general agreement that a new concept of a sound individualism is in the air, and needs to be captured and formulated.

In another camp, with a more religious and traditional orientation, this something new is being called, not the new individualism, but the "new

---

[36] *Op., cit.*, p. 116.

conservatism," whose hero in social, political, and religious thought is Edmund Burke, in his *Reflections on the Revolution in France*.[37] Russell Kirk's recent *The Conservative Mind*[38] is the bible of the present-day group of new conservatives.[39] Their outlook is comparable to Toynbee's in history (in his middle period) and to Eliot's in literature. (Eliot is known to have said that he is an Anglo-Catholic in religion, a royalist in polities, and a classicist in literature.)

These theorists, most of whom are in the United States, find the depth-psychology approach objectionable, but they share with those psychologists the concern to reach an adequate concept of individuality and freedom and the conviction that "reason" is hedged in on all sides by factors that make it fairly impotent. Like Burke, they see the well-being of the individual as thoroughly dependent on institutions, the more hallowed by tradition the better; and the political institution of the State is subordinate to the religious one of the

---

[37] London: J. Dodsley, 1790.

[38] *The Conservative Mind, from Burke to Santayana* (Chicago: H. Regnery Co., 1953).

[39] Others in or associated with this movement are: Walter Lippmann, Clinton Rossiter, and Francis Wilson. See F. Wilson, *The Case for Conservatism* (Seattle: University of Washington Press, 1951). Also, Peter R. E. Viereck, *Conservatism from John Adams to Churchill* (Princeton: D. Van Nostrand Co., Inc., 1956), a good short survey of the whole movement since Burke.

Church, all under God. The wise individual will be institution-directed. The rational intelligence of the individual is suspect, and is demoted to the position of servant of something higher, in which service is perfect freedom. "The rationalist or liberal frames his decisions in accordance with some theory derived from an abstract notion of universal truth; the conservative takes into consideration an extremely wide range of concrete acts. . . ."[40] The new conservative, in short, eschews rational constructions in favor of devout action under spiritual regulation from on high, manifest in crucial events and interpreted by an institutional elite. The recrudescence of this sort of spiritual elitism favors *some* form of aristocracy. (Compare Indian thought on this count.) It should be noted that not all the new conservatives stress religious fundamentals. For example, Walter Lippmann, pundit of the *New York Times,* has taken, on the whole, a more secular stand in favor of a new conservative view of man's good, making the theory look more like a new humanism. *All* of them fear the possible "tyranny of the majority," which threatens most in democracy as usually conceived. And it is this that has created the need for a new concept of individualism — beyond even the best insights of

---

[40] Viereck, *op. cit.*, p. 108.

Dewey's once-influential social philosophy. The New Conservatism at present is itself not widely influential—it appeals mainly to church and university leaders and professors of political science—except as an expression (not a cause) of the world-wide worry about the place of reason in human affairs.

Some of the omissions in this brief survey will be made good in the general interpretations and the comparisons that follow. To this task, including reflections on the bearing of the theories on actual social practices in the West, I now turn.

C. Beyond Ethics

There is a position already magnificently outlined which sets the stage for my final consideration about the present moral mentality of East and West. This is the one that F. S. C Northrop takes in his *The Meeting of East and West*,[41] and especially his *The Taming of the Nations*.[42]

---

[41] New York: The Macmillan Co., 1946.
[42] New York: The Macmillan Co., 1952.

Northrop's position is too well known to call for elaboration here. Let me be brief. There is, for him, a very general distinction between the genius of the East and that of the West. The mind of the Orient it intuitive, spiritually sensitive to the "undifferentiated continuum," as ultimate reality. So, the Eastern sage will tend to void the personal identity of his ego in the vastness of the real, and not to make much of differences in theories and rules of conduct, all of which are superficial. To achieve this, one must not be preoccupied with activity in the framework of ideas, desires, and goals of action. Calling the blessed result thus arrived at either Being or Non-Being makes only a terminological difference—Brahman, Nirvana, Tao, Jen. But, moral or ethical striving presupposes this framework of unreal distinctions. So, ethics and morality will be tentative, to be finally dissolved in the solvent of the Absolute Vastness. There can be no ultimate concern to take a definite ethical stand. The moral function of a wise man, in this view, will be that of the mediator seeking compromise, without himself having a fixed ethical position.

The Western mind is logical. Its genius is the Word, the "theoretically given logos of the classical

West."[43] In its pristine purity and first intention, this is the principle of universalism in theoretical constructions, which are the fruits of ideational intelligence. In principle, there is one true theory, one law, one institution (political or religious) for all men. There has been a fragmentation of this by unfortunate mistakes in the West: dogmatic absolutism instead of constitutionalism in politics, half-baked Protestantism instead of genuine Catholicism in religion, misconceptions in philosophies leading to a pluralism of conflicting theories of Nature and man, etc. This has been the "fall from grace," symbolized by the story of the Garden of Eden and its misappropriated Tree of Knowledge.

To be moral, under this aegis, is to know and to respect in action the Law Universal. This taxes both the intellect and the will of the ethical person more than his intuitive sensibilities. Anyway, this is the characteristic *tendency* of the Western mind in moral action. Moral obligation is a fixed and ultimate thing.

---

[43] *The Taming of the Nations*, p. 226. See also chap. V.

Northrop's conception of Eastern morality as provisional is underwritten by our representative from India, Mahadevan, both in his essay of a decade ago at the East-West Conference[44] and in his "Beyond Ethics" (1953).[45] "One cannot attain the goal [of life] so long as one remains merely moral."[46] Being moral is too closely tied in with the intellectual machinery of theoretical constructs and the drive of desires influencing the will. To be sure, there are duties to be fulfilled, but with as little desire as possible and with the sustained realization that true guidance comes from a supra-moral source, not from the etiquette or the imperatives of moral intelligence. From a different angle, a Zen Buddhist concurs: "In Buddha-mind there is nothing good, nothing bad; nothing to be called right, nothing to be called wrong."[47]

Now, as I take on the role of moderator, I first remember with gratitude Radhakrishnan's warning that all "immense simplifications of the complicated

---

[44] In Charles A. Moore, ed., *Essays in East-West Philosophy* (Honolulu: University of Hawaii Press, 1951), pp. 317-355.

[45] Mahadevan, "Beyond Ethics," in T. M. P. Mahadevan, et al., eds., *The Indian Philosophical Congress*. Silver Jubilee Volume (Madras: Indian Philosophical Congress, 1950), pp. 43-54.

[46] In Moore, ed., *Essays in East-West Philosophy*, p. 322.

[47] Nyogen Senzaki, "Mentorgarten Dialogue," *Chicago Review*, XII, No. 2 (Summer, 1958), 37-40.

pattern of reality are misleading."[48] Then I bare my forehead to the light of what seems to be the dawn of a new philosophical entente between East and West, and proceed.

I find Northrop's metaphysical scheme too general to serve as an instrument of exposition or correction that does justice to either the Occidental or the Oriental mind. But he has tempered this by recognizing the diversities on both sides of the fence, and this description of the mentality of the East with respect to morality or ethics is significant and true. (Whether this is *explained* by his metaphysics of theoretic (determinate) and aesthetic (indeterminate) components of reality remains, however, an interesting question.) There is little doubt that, according to the Oriental view, though man is *in* a stratum of ethical being and action, he is not essentially *of* it. The result of our second East-West conference may seem to deny this; it does not really. The Asian is provisional and compromising in his moral conduct. He is head, shoulders, and heart above the plane of *ethical* concern, while his nether parts are caught in its substructure of *karma-yoga*. In this connection, it appears that Charles A.

---

[48] S. Radhakrishnan, *Eastern Religions and Western Thought* (2nd. ed., London: Oxford University Press, 1940, p. 74.

Moore's argument to the effect that the Easterner is fundamentally moral is an over-statement,[49] while Northrop, backed by Mahadevan, is nearer the truth.

To unsnarl this complex issue, I must conclude by distinguishing the various ways of getting and being beyond ethics, in theory and social practice, noticing cases both in the Eastern and in the Western camps. Surprising parallels and differences will emerge, with some suggestion of a new over-all concept of morality. These ways are:

A. We might notice, first, in passing, a way to get beyond ethics that is trivial in some respects, and becomes a bore if dwelt with too long. This is the way of meta-ethics, the study of the use or function of ethical expressions. But we must remember that even this movement, cavalierly overlooked by the tradition-minded philosopher, was and is motivated by a question of cardinal philosophical importance moving us all, namely, the problem of the place of reason in moral experience, thought, and action. The new language-philosophers of the Oxford ilk make this explicit, in a more profound consideration

---

[49] Moore, ed., *Essays in East-West Philosophy*, chap. XXII.

than that of the logical positivists. This has already been suggested. Also, such an approach, conscious of the various ways expressions mean even within the single area of moral judgment and valuation, clears the path for more progress in substantive ethics or ethics proper, the study of the non-linguistic conditions of morality. Metaphysicians, mystics, and theologians have themselves suggested *some* such distinctions from the beginning. Remember, too, that the findings of the new meta-ethicists do not support subjectivism in moral theory or the old relativism—though neither does it aid and abet traditional rationalism or objectivism.

B. Then there is the way of existentialism, with its metaphysics of the vacuum in which lonely men exist (*Existenz*), act, and choose, *before* essence and order are realized by creative fiat, under no cosmic regulation. Schopenhauer's vision of the irrational will, hungrily and desperately "objectifying" itself to get something to cope with and to depend on for provisional satisfactions, provides a classical frame for the current existentialist picture. This existentialist consciousness or mood is nihilistic, in which *everything* is provisional, including certainly the ethical concern with its objectives. The spirit of Hīnayāna Buddhism is conspicuously akin to this, as also is Taoism on some counts. All this, of course, does not mean that men will not take any ethical action. It means, rather, that they will act under concocted rules. The religious or Kierkegaardian existentialists provide a transcendent principle in God, the approach to which, however, is thoroughly irrational and supra-moral—a notion that brings Tillich into this camp. In fact, Tillich's manner of thinking and speaking about this suggests that man's final and highest comprehension places him above even religious theism—something that any good Hegelian (or Buddhist) would assert. So, one's ethical (to say nothing of religious) procedure is indeed quite tentative. A definite ethical regulation is not to be had, or a specifically ethical theory. The human spirit is left as a pulsation between Being and Non-Being, with the "courage to be" as its only moral directive.

C. Mysticism's way of transcending ethics is classically exhibited in the East, and on this I have already touched. The metaphor may be either that of up or down. The former I have already used—head and heart above, etc.— as have most of the great Oriental mystics. But the below-ethics picture is also powerfully suggestive and frequently used. The image then is of sinking into the universal deep, and of dissolving the limitations of the finite ego there—though this will be something like "pouring milk into milk." The experience of sinking into a profound sleep is a favorite example. In the Upanisads, Āruni says to his son, "Now, when one is sound asleep; composed, serene, and knows no dream. . . . That is Brahman.[50] This has the true ring of any consistent and final mysticism, and carries with it the suggestion of a condition beyond the wakeful and strident concerns of the ethical consciousness of the individual-in-action. Of course, there is the paradoxical notion of the possibility of being wisely asleep even while one acts, in a kind of trance of detachment, and there is some genuine wisdom in practicing this. But, even then, the point of the mystic is that there is something ultimate one had better keep in mind if he is not to become the slave of ethical concern. And this, too, as I shall finally argue, is important to realize. But with a different emphasis.

D. The metaphor of depth reminds us of depth psychology and its way of getting beyond ethics. In its Freudian form, the theory is clearly distinguishable from mysticism. Its method requires

---

[50] S. Radhakrishnan and Charles A. Moore, eds., *A Source Book in Indian Philosophy* (Princeton: Princeton University Press, 1957), p. 68.

it to eschew *normative* standards of evaluation and moral judgment in favor of a clinical one. What psychoanalysis does is simply to uncover causes or motives of the conscious behavior of the ego, sandwiched between the dark subliminal Id beneath and the Super-Ego above, whose social pressure tames or civilizes the beast below as much as possible, in the wakeful personal performance of the individual. As Riesman said, these psychologists cure sick people, without exactly knowing what the norm of health is—and without meaning to make moral judgments or develop an ethical theory. In the Jungian version, the concepts (archetypal images, etc.) become even more metaphysical, and so the color is more congenial both to religion and to a mystical theory, though still without explicit bearing on what one *ought* to do in an ethical sense of the term. Zimmer's interpretation of the philosophical mind of India in these terms is a significant example.[51]

E. What might be called evolutionary-goal philosophies also tend to get beyond ethics, in a characteristic way. And I do not mean primarily the old Darwinian and Spencerian naturalism, as formulated in Huxley's *Evolution and Ethics*

---

[51] Heinrich Zimmer, *Philosophies of India* (New York: Pantheon Books, 1956).

(translated into Chinese in 1898).[52] Nietzsche's case is much more significant, and so is that of communism under the spell of Marx and Lenin. It is the analysis of such more ideological and romantic cases that discloses what we now need most to do as moral philosophers, in a meeting of Eastern and Western minds.

To make this final crucial point, I must first remind you of the grand distinction, in the history of moral philosophy, between respect-for-law theories (deontic), on the one hand, and value-realization (axiological and telic), on the other. Generally speaking, the former have been "formalistic," stressing ethical rectitude even where this is at the expense of valuable goals that might have been realized without the ethical restrictions. They have defined duty as the requirement of conformity to rules or forms of *correct* procedure, in a law-abiding spirit and for the sake of moral character-building. The value-realization theories have, on the other hand, subordinated such rectitude (rightness, righteousness, virtue) to the goods of life or at least to a good something, defining duty primarily in the light of attaining the latter (the "good" vs. the

---

[52] T. H. Huxley, *Evolution and Ethics, and Other Essays* (New York: D. Appleton and Company, 1896).

"right"). Thus does the *ethical* (right) appear antithetical to the valuable (good), and the question of duty or what one ought to do becomes problematic, sometimes agonizingly so in specific cases. That the right and the good are independent and occasionally incompatible principles of duty is not just an appearance. It is a fact, structuring the theater of human existence, generating there the tragic sense of life and the penitent appeal to a transcendental source for forgiveness and a final redemption beyond our power as human beings. When Gautama Buddha left his wife and child for the sake of the *good*, he violated a rule of *right* action. He broke a promise. He was being unethical, which he sadly sensed, though it was his genius to fulfill his duty in but one of its dimensions, the axiological. Attempts to make one of these principles derivative from, or to define one in terms of, the other have failed. So, J. S. Mill fails in his conception of the foundations of *right* conduct (duty) under ethical rules, by a too exclusive featuring of the goal of striving—the *good* as the general happiness. He was reacting against Kant, who made the opposite mistake of leaving valuable consequences (goals) of action completely out of the consideration of dutiful conduct.

I am suggesting that moral philosophy has two distinct, irreducible, and co-ordinate principles to keep in view while developing a concept of Duty (this time with a capital). Questions about the *good* or the valuable, and the logic of value-judgments, are about a property or state of being as the goal of conduct. Questions about the *right* or the ethical, and the logic of ethical judgments, concern the imperatives of correct procedure in the attainment of the goal, to the point of ignoring the latter if necessary to ethical righteousness. And Duty is to be conceived and defined by reference to the demands of *both* distinct sets of imperatives: ethical imperatives and value-imperatives, there being no pre-established harmony between them on the plane of actual human striving ("right" and "good," with "ought" as the tantalizing connective).

Let as look at the communist mentality and practice in the framework of this suggestion. There the goal-oriented value-imperatives dominate, and duty is conceived mainly under this head, at the expense of the ethical. This is the communist's way of getting beyond *ethics*—not beyond values. This ideology plainly favors amoralism (in the form of non-ethical concern) in conduct, even explicitly in some of its literature (e.g., *The Mandarins*, and

Arthur Koestler's *Darkness at Noon*) invoking evolution and revolution in support of a swift and ruthless drive toward the realization of values. And the ultimate goal is pictured as a social condition in which the need for institutionalized ethical regulation will have withered away completely. When men are quite good, they are quite beyond ethics; and they are eventually going to be quite good. Ethical considerations should not be allowed to slow up progress toward that goal.

    This is a lopsided philosophy of duty, nourished by a sentimental and optimistic metaphysics of human nature. Human nature demands that action be both ethical and valuable, though this does produce tension and conflict in sensitive moral experience. Being a man can be *defined* by this dual demand. The recognition of either set of imperatives in the human situation may tend to minimize the other, yet the total demand of Duty makes both mandatory. To operate too exclusively under just one principle or the other tends to make monsters of men. The puritan mind[53] has been guilty of the mistake of conceiving duty too much in the dimension of ethical rectitude under a

---

[53] See Herbert W. Schneider, *The Puritan Mind* (Ann Arbor: University of Michigan Press, 1957) for an excellent, sympathetic account.

Kantian pattern, while the communist mentality has sinned in the direction of value-realization beyond ethics. The classic lament of Boris Pasternak's *Dr. Zhivago*[54] is to the point. Larissa sadly notices Strelnikov's face become an abstract symbol of an impersonal collective drive toward a valuable goal which The Party aims to realize, flouting ethical or moral considerations of persons as individuals along the way. The communist does this with the sense of doing his duty. And he cannot be *simply* refuted. He is doing his duty (little d), but not his Duty (capital), which requires more than the urgent and sincere reaching for values. It demands also that the action taken to realize them be ethical, even where this slows progress toward the goal. The rules governing this matter of human life-and-death make a sort of ultimate game of living wisely. You can win only by obeying the dual requirement of Duty. It is rather like another game that can be imagined. Suppose there are roses (values) in a box with a small aperture (ethical restrictions). One has a short time to get the roses out through the opening, and he wins the game who gets most out without injury to the flowers. The game of Duty is like that: there are values which can be possessed only under the restriction of ethical imperatives, such as prohibit

---

[54] Max Hayward and Manya Harari, trans. (New York: Pantheon Books, 1958).

lying, cheating, slandering. Above all, they prohibit using individual persons as mere means to ends, howsoever valuable the ends. Disregarding this rule deforms the values that are too ruthlessly possessed.

As Mahadevan has said, the mind of India is value-oriented in practically all its thinking. "Indian philosophy is essentially a philosophy of values."[55] But what this means to the mystical Indian is different in a very significant respect from what it means to a Chinese communist who was conditioned by the Neo-Confucianism of, say, K'ang Yu-wei (of the latter half of the nineteenth century) to receive the Marxist idea of a secular, social goal as the final value, the supreme good.[56] What the Indian philosophy of values calls the final or supreme value redeems it from requiring harsh treatment of individuals. It is, rather, a compassionate plea for a higher mode of being, transcending the painful or sorrowful distinction between the ethical and the valuable.[57] In this light, if we still call the Most High "good" or "valuable," we

---

[55] Moore, ed., *Essays in East-West Philosophy*, p. 317.

[56] O. Briere, *Fifty Years of Chinese Philosophy*. L. G. Thompson, trans. (London: George Allen & Unwin Ltd., 1956).

[57] P. T. Raju refers to the Most High as "the Great Spirit . . . transcending his relations to matter and society," which nicely marks off the Indian philosophy from the communistic, though both are goal-oriented in *some* sense. In Moore, ed., *Essays in East-West Philosophy*, p. 227.

must realize that we are using these terms not in their ordinary signification but as Spinoza used them, in application to the Absolute. Such meaning as they then retain, if any, is open only to mystical or religious insight, and closed to philosophical *statement.*

Spinoza also called this human wisdom at its height the "intellectual love of God." I suggest that the voice of Duty at its transcendent apex, above the ramification into the two little voices of ethical and valuational imperatives, which regulate us here below, is the voice of Love moving us to that compassionate, trans-rational understanding of one another which tempers the tragic complications into which men are born, and among which they live and die. Our ultimate task, as philosophers of East and West, is the dedicated study of this concept of Duty, especially in its tantalizing dual requirement that men live with a respect for both values *and* ethics—since this is how we must live as men, if not as gods. The formula that respects and resolves this duality is the one that, on the whole, the Western mind in moral action is *trying* to abide by, without a clear understanding of what the formula is. The West is *not* content, as the East *tends* to be despite its demurrers, with the solution of salvation by transcendence of physical existence. We Westerners continue to love *this* world, though our lives have in recent decades become somewhat desperate. This-worldliness is what, by and large, distinguishes us from our Eastern colleagues. We like the expression of a modern Western painter [Renoir] who loved colorful things: "This earth . . . the paradise of gods"—though hell encroach upon and darken it as it quite certainly does. Or, a line from Handel's *Messiah* may do, if the mood is religious: "Though worms destroy my body, yet *in my flesh* shall I see God." To the Westerner, bodies are wonderful, though a source of corruption. He wants a formula that saves him in the flesh, while bringing his spirit to full flower. And he believes that no Easterner really means to reject such a formula. The real problem is to find it.

31.

This concept of "game"—remember my little game of roses in the box—is getting a thorough work-out nowadays. Not only in economics and in other technological applications—"theory of games," as it's called—but also in the philosophy of language, thanks to Wittgenstein. In the latter area, the notion has become one of "language games." But what this turns out to mean does not suggest having fun. Along with the notion that using language is in effect to be playing various games with its phrases, each of these being defined by distinctive logical rules, goes the notion that language is our "form of life." We come to life, we realize ourselves as human beings, in speaking. This makes the matter an affair of ultimate concern that the game be played well—and won. As the great mountain climber climbs Everest, not for fun, but to realize himself as a man. To lose this venture is to die, literally if by accident, spiritually if by failure to make the ascent.

But there is a distinction between a "game" and a "sport" that I must recognize before I can make the point I have in mind about the central activity of life called moral conduct. And it is this activity, not primarily the overlapping linguistic activity of speaking, that I am focusing on here. Is this more like a game, or like a sport? Or a blend of these?

A clear-cut case of something that is a game and *not* a sport is, say, chess or cards. One "sits down" to play a game. (We say, "play a game"; we never say, "play a sport.") The moves that are made here and that count, and that are rule-regulated, involve not the physique of the player but the pieces—pawns, trumps, etc. If it is chess and the player is a real champion, he may sit before the fireplace reading a newspaper with his back to the chess board, telling his opponent what moves to make with the pieces. The rules say nothing against such conduct of the player.

But if it is a sport, the conduct of the sportsman is of the essence. Not only in the sense of fair play, but primarily with a view to himself in skillful action. He "engages" in the activity that defines the sport; he does not "play" the sport as he does the game. The way *he* moves, meaning his body-mind and its members, is what counts. In the game, it was the way he moved the *pieces* with his fingertips if it is chess. Thus the essence of a game is given by giving the rules governing moves of the pieces. Not so for a sport, such as skiing or swimming or mountain climbing. Of course, there are controls on such activities, but not in the form of rules unless the sports are competitive or social. If they are, then the term "games" also applies to them, as in the case of the Olympic games. But, given the rules in such an application and your having learned—memorized—them, you will still not know how to swim or ski. So, insofar as a sport as an activity to be participated in is concerned, you do not give its essence by giving the rules governing it in its social or competitive forms. The activity is of the essence, something *you* do with your whole body, something you may have learned to do quite well before learning the rules. One certainly can't say that of a game that is not a sport, like cards. But you can say it of, for example, tennis, since this is both a game and a sport from the beginning. It is nothing without the rules, and nothing without the skillful activity enlisting the whole agent, pitted against the opponent player.

Now, as for the "controls" that are on the sport as such, how do they differ from "rules"? Well, the main difference is that controls are naturally built in on the side of the situation, and acquired in the form of skills on the side of the sportsman. Skiing, for example. Here the controls are the contours and slopes of the run, the texture of the snow, the relative velocity of the wind the skier leans into and adjusts his skis to for the long jumps. These are built into the natural situation of the performance. The athlete-in-action "observes" this set of factors. Then there are the controls that the skier exerts, so to speak, from within. These he acquires by practice. Given both sorts of controls, the sport may be made social or competitive ("conventional") by the introduction of rules, involving artificially induced complications among the controls to increase the degree of difficulty of the performance, as an occasion for exhibiting skill that now is subject to a sort of measure, as it was not in the state of nature. The activity then becomes both a sport and a game.

I come at last to the application I want to make of all this talk about games and sports. Is there some analogy, perhaps a revealing one, with the activity called moral conduct? Is it significant to say of this that it is a kind of sport, or game, or both at once? Perhaps more one than the other though a blend of both?

Putting the question this way may suggest a misconception that must be demolished at once. It suggests that moral conduct is a specific sort of activity, coordinate with other such activities and to be distinguished from them as they are from one another. This notion would be a complete mistake, the notion that now I engage in tennis, now in teaching, now in writing a book, and then, for a change, in moral conduct. One is moral or immoral in *any* activity deliberately engaged in, even in activities that one may have been pressured to participate in by what Hume would call the "gentle force" of customs, so long as the actions involved can properly be called human acts, not just natural processes or happenings. Therefore moral conduct must be thought of as a second-order activity that characterizes first-order activities—perhaps less misleadingly— by saying that any human act or activity is moral or not according as it is or is not regulated in a certain way, where the regulation consists of controls or rules. Whether it is rules or controls that count here, or both, is precisely what I want to find out. And what they are.

32.

My general idea is that the regulations governing moral conduct are of two sorts: the "controls," which are the anticipated consequences of actions deliberately taken, together with the situation of the actions, on the one hand, and, on the other, the "rules" that declare which such actions, as practical means to the ends, are ethical or unethical, right or wrong, prescribing or at least permitting the former and proscribing the latter. In this dual framework, a bit of conduct is said to be moral to the degree that what is realized by it (the consequence) is "good" or valuable, *and* the action taken to realize this is "right" or ethical. Thus moral conduct is two-dimensional, and the concept of moral conduct is broader than the concept of *ethical* conduct. Strictly speaking, an action is ethical if it accords with the rule of right action that applies to that kind of action, and it can have this merit without being the means to a good or valuable material consequence. It might even have a bad consequence and still be ethical in this restricted sense of "ethical." But, on this count of failing to realize a value, it will not be *moral.* Similarly, an unethical action may have a very good result. It will thereby be "a good" thing to do, but not "the right" thing to do. Strictly speaking, this use of "good" as applied to an action that functions as means to an end is derivative. The action reflects the goodness or badness, value or disvalue, of its consequence. In itself it is right or wrong, as the consequence is, in itself, good or bad.

An illustration of all this is the case of a young scientist who promises his dying friend to be a father to the dying man's little son. Later, as his genius possesses him, the scientist is completely absorbed by his creative work and neglects more and more the growing boy. He sadly realizes that he has broken a promise, in favor of the valuable consequences of his activity. His conduct is thus immoral on the ethical count, the count of rectitude, while it is justified teleologically on the count of something good accomplished. The ethical requirement or *rule*, "Keep promises," is violated, while the *control*—the good consequence criterion—is satisfied. Thus the answer to the question, is his conduct moral? is yes-and-no. But to the question, is it ethical? the answer is a simple no. Is it valuable? Yes, certainly, anyway, with respect to *this* good consequence.

Now, as Aristotle and others have pointed out, one who consistently acts with respect for the ethical rules develops a good character, this being a set of dispositions to continue acting ethically. Moreover, such rule-compliant action will have other good consequences, such as building confidence in others. Notice that here I am speaking of the "good consequences" of *ethical* action, to be distinguished as a special set from good consequences in the moral general sense including such *things* as good ships, good cities, and good works of art—or a good thermonuclear bomb. These latter might all be realized by action in violation of ethical rules, unlike the former. It is important to keep this distinction between kinds of consequences in mind when we get to the question of justification of *ethical* imperatives and the ethical conduct obedient to them. The only consequences that can count or be appealed to in such a justification are the special set having to do with the person or the character of the agent, and the characters or persons of other people affected by the action. The reason why such a justification cannot properly go on to mention the other good "things" in general is that so many of them are produced by people who are ethically defective. In fact, in many such cases the production of the goods would have been either delayed or perhaps permanently put off, had the agent decided to proceed ethically right down the line. Remember the above example of the scientist. Keeping his promise would have tended to perfect his person or his character and that of the boy, ethically speaking, but at the expense of his work as a scientist. Think also of Gaugin, who broke his ethical commitments to his family and society to perfect his work as an artist.

Yeats has presented this as a standing and tragic predicament of being a man, in his poem "The Choice." One must choose between the perfection of his person or character on the one hand, and the perfection of his "work" on the other. Here, again, the artist speaks, out of a cosmic sense that there may be something better than being ethical, in some circumstances. Some valuable work to be done, at ethical costs. Of course, most people will not feel this tragic conflict because most people do not hear a calling to do something specially significant in a big way. They are the comfortable and happy people, Aristotle to the contrary notwithstanding who made it look as if the great man is even happier, as if being a whole man and a genius at the same time were quite compatible. Actually, it is the little man who has the happy privilege of being a whole man. To overlook this is to miss the tragic inner conflict in one who is exceptionally great in a certain direction, either towards personal character-building—becoming a saint in interpersonal relations—or in the direction of the making of good "things." One is never *very* good in both these directions at once, since the activity of one sort involves sacrifices for the other sort, for the exceptionally great man. Jesus and Gantama Buddha were like this and built wonderful *persons* but they produced no good *things*. Whereas Pascal, da Vinci, and Edison produced good *things* but are not known as character-builders.

33.

The rewards of ethical rectitude, the essence of which is careful or loving consideration of persons including one's own, are thus thought to be had in the next life or in heaven, not in this world. Chastity, poverty and obedience are properly the key words here. Of course, this is to construe rewards as good *things*, the production or possession of which in this life is not at all necessarily connected with being an ethical man. Kant emphasized this with an annoying ferocity, in his deontology of morals. The mighty opposite of this position is the teleological emphasis on realizing secular goods, as in Mill's—and Marx's—morality of utility. Health, wealth, and happiness, and the constellation of good things that go along with these.

How happiness figures among the good consequences is problematic for these philosophies, including Aristotle's. All of them agree that it is not exactly a good "thing" among others, coordinate with them. They also agree that it is, however, a consequence of conducting oneself in a certain way, as are the other good—and bad—things. But for Aristotle this conduct, this very activity, though it at first aims at happiness as an end, itself becomes happiness, when it has had time to gather around it the virtues as right dispositions and the good "things" of life. *Then* to continue to be active "in accordance with" these dispositions and their fruits is to be happy. This is perhaps the best conception of human happiness in the world, since it avoids the sentimentalist's fallacy of identifying it with a sort of "pathological" state or feeling, as a consequence of moral conduct, the sort of mistake Mill and Kant made. Having made this mistake, Kant, emphasizing ethical rectitude, had to deny that happiness considerations are important in ethical deliberation, and Mill had to lapse into an ungrounded optimism about the nice connection in general between ethical rectitude and being happy as its result, that pleasant feeling just above contentment and just below rapture.

But there seems to be something wrong even with Aristotle's conception that simply *identifies* being happy with being active in a certain way. It is indeed the activity that counts for most, but it is so often clear that, even during periods of such engagement, what is experienced or realized is relief or satisfaction, and that both of these must be distinguished from the activity itself *and* from happiness. Consider Van Gogh's case. A torment of yearning for an activity that would replace an intolerable idleness, then the fever of the activity itself that he felt was consuming him, out of which he would anxiously emerge to envy the happy, sociable people around him. The relief and satisfaction of creative work, yes, but not happiness. This notion of satisfaction without pleasure or happiness is an important one in the adequate description of the "good" life of the great man, who may save others but not himself. It has not been sufficiently recognized. The recognition puts a big dent in hedonism, and disinclines one even to equate Aristotle's *eudaimonia*, the activity itself, with happiness.

34.

There are legends and myths dramatizing Yeats' point about the tragic choice. The person dies unto the perfection of the work, whether it is the work of perfecting other persons by exemplary living and teaching, or the work of producing and perfecting good things. The motive is a compelling love, for persons in the one case and for things in the other. In either case the lover sacrifices himself, for the sake of the perfection of the work—the beloved. Something like this is the meaning of the crucifixion, the cross being the symbol of self-sacrificial love.

But this message is commonly misunderstood as a prescription for ordinary people to "love God and do as they please." It is, rather, a description of the way of life of a great man. Jesus did not die to liberate the rank and file of people—the sheep of His hand—from the moral law with its ethical requirements, though he himself, as the greatest lover of persons, had to do some flouting of such rules in this theory and his practice. (His treatment of his own mother and father, for example.) So his performance was paradoxical. The purpose of his self-sacrificial death is, rather, to incline people to obey the commandments including the eloquent little ones in the Sermon on the Mount. The salvation of ordinary people consists precisely in this, that they be persuaded to be regulated by such ethical restrictions on their impulsive animal natures, on their drives toward goals of action. This is for the sheep—and the wolves. The controls on the *shepherd* are something else. *These* controls are not on the rank and file of people. To exempt *them* from the ethical rules is simply to give them license.

As for the great lovers of good things, not of persons, again there is this excuse for not being too ethical. A certain overriding of interpersonal obligations is occasionally necessary for the realization of good things. Hegel dramatized this in his metaphysics of the Absolute pursuing its own cosmic, concealed ends, in the course of which action many ethical rules are ruthlessly broken, as niceties or proprieties the observance of which would slow up progress towards the great goal. From the Absolute's point of view, such constraints are more honored in the breach than in the observance, relative to the good end to be achieved by the unethical action. This notion has sparked the "morality" of communism, which plays up the value of the great final goal at the expense of ethical restrictions *en route*.

35.

Let me get back to my impressions of the political consciousness in my century. They jell into a single impression that may be taken as a sort of implicit definition of "political consciousness." Of course, the aim is to tie this in with considerations of morality, and finally to imagine a setting in which the tragedy of The Choice will be somewhat mitigated. My impression so far of morality is that it makes a dual demand, to act ethically with concern for persons and for the states of character that are the consequences of such action on the one hand, and, on the other, to act with a view to realizing good things, taking "things" here in a broad sense that includes not only the necessities and conveniences of wholesome living but also such ethereal things as works of art (beautiful or expressive things) and true conceptions or theories (knowledge). So far, my picture presents the personal and the "reified" sets of consequences as jointly realizable in a small way in the inconspicuous performance of the average man proceeding towards routine goods under ethical rules. But for a man with the capacity and dedication of genius, not only will the pursuit of one set of consequences usually exclude the pursuit of the other, but in either case such conspicuous performance will occasionally exclude ethical considerations, towards oneself in the former case (self-sacrifice unto death for others), and towards both oneself and others in the second, in the realization of good "things."

So, in talking about the politically conscious man, one must not forget the distinctions that are to be made according to the degree of greatness of the man in that respect, whether he is a political leader or just another John Doe.

My impression of what political consciousness is conforms in fundamental respects to Pasternak's as expressed in his *Dr. Zhivago*. So let me next give you a glimpse of the main characters in this novel, with comments to follow. I take the account almost verbatim from notes I made after reading Pasternak.

Larissa, also called Lara, is a symbol of *natural* beauty and purity, tinctured with the erotic and close to corruption— the paradox of the spontaneously or immediately lovable as essentially rash, unclean, confusing, and evil. (Remember Thomas Mann's point of the *Magic Mountain*, the heroine with dirty fingernails; and the theme throughout of the affinity of love, disease and death.) Then there is Komarovsky, old and powerful with a this-worldly lure, symbolizing the insensitive and acquisitive side, whom Zhivago senses will get Larissa, as he finally does. Strelnikov (Pavel or Pasha Antipov) is Larissa's husband, weak and lovable at first, then becoming a symbol of the hard integrity and order that a fanatically determined attachment to The Cause of the Party produces. This, the Revolution in its aftermath of consolidation, galvanizes and finally damns him. His face becomes abstract in the end, a mere label on the demonic fury which, as an inhuman abstraction, motivates him into military leadership. So he becomes pretentious, theatrical and hollow in personal and domestic relationships. He shoots himself in the end when Zhivago tells him of Lara's dream of how she and Pasha were at first, when he was still an individual though a weak one, in their home and family life, and how she would have crawled back—her own words—on her knees to *that* life with him in the first natural light of human love.

Zhivago (Yurii, Yura) is the profound spiritual lover of Russia and of Life which he feels are not to be forcefully manipulated and molded. He is an intuitionist, fatalist, moved by a religious conception of history (evolution) and destiny; such a "myth" is man's making and hope. This was at first the glorious motive even of the Russian Revolution which however was soon emptied of this spirit in favor of formulas of collective living under force and inhuman penalties for deviations. (Koestler said something like this in his *Darkness at Noon*.) Brotherhood had become enforced togetherness and soulless collaboration because love of one another as individuals had ceased to be the motive, replaced by love of The Cause. Zhivago favors the "logic of the emotions." He is a symbol of genuine intimacy with people and nature, and it is this penchant that detaches him from the concerted and convulsed actions of regimented herds of hollow men whose humanity is thus destroyed. Yurii falls in love with Larissa. He loves her first, last, and infinitely, with the instability and sickness for ethics that goes along with that. His own wife Tonia is a pale image beside that of Larissa. Tonia senses that Lara is her opposite—Tonia the principle of simplicity and fidelity (ethical health), Lara of confusion and eventual undoing, with her natural spontaneity. Zhivago fears and hates the chemistry, the sweat and germs, of Lara's body, as symptomatic of Komarovsky's destructive kind, demonic, evil, yet fascinating because of the closeness of these to Life in its most lovable form. (Remember *Dr. Faustus.*) The rowan tree is a symbol of this: life fused with desperate and dangerous love. Yurii dies of a heart ailment caused by the moral disorders of his society. He was an excellent, intuitive diagnostician of troubles, physical and spiritual, and he knew what was wrong with himself.

36.

What bearing has all this on the nature of the political consciousness, letting "political" here have the connection it popularly has with "politics"? What occurs first to one is that it is a sort of cause-consciousness where the cause consists of certain effects ("ends") to be realized under the management of a political leader, whose instruments are persons. That is, persons are treated by the ruling faction as having instrumental value, the measure of which is how efficiently they are related to the cause. And this tends to become the measure of their value as persons. Thus is the notion of the *intrinsic* value of persons as such undermined.

Such consciousness tends to crystallize and take over in situations where there is a failure in personal relations; *i.e.*, in unethical situations—situations in which the protest that individuals are being unfairly dealt with goes unheeded. It is in such circumstances that the political remedy for this suggests itself and seems most commendable. So the "people's democracy" emerges to rectify things under the absolute management of the Party. The

Party itself is constituted and defined by the "man of the people" who becomes the Leader. This sounds very much like Plato's reflection and judgment on democracy and tyranny, and it is reminiscent of many similar anxieties of later philosophers, the latest among whom are the religious existentialists, e.g., Gabriel Marcel with his worries about technological collectivization.

But it is noteworthy in our time that the growth of the political consciousness is attended by the dissolution of many institutions or norms that have no obvious connection with the political. In religion, for example, a new brand of theologians proclaim that God is dead, that He has "emptied himself" into the "body of humanity" (Altizer). The suggestion is that it is the people, The People, who are finally sacred, and that individuals are to sacrifice, and be sacrificed, to this new god, The People, under the regulation of the leader who is the technologized brain of this Body Politic. His closest henchmen are those who install computers to automate the management of The People. Of course, the new theologians leave this part of the story untold.

In art, a rash of new practices is breaking out that shatter the old forms and norms, the unconscious aim being to dissolve any standards that might offer resistance to the overall political end, or to reduce the art-world to a state of dependence-for-direction on Technological Intelligence. Thus, "op" (optical) artists, relying on technological know-how to produce dizziness in the beholders of their works, explicitly declare that these celebrate the emergence of the new deity Physical Science. And other artists are hanging screwdrivers and metrical devices on the surfaces of their canvases. Then there are the mobiles of junked parts.

In business the slogan-word is "new." It has become a hazard to like yesterday's product. Today it is televised as new, and some new twist is indeed given it. Thus is the need for innovation at all costs driven home, and one is made to feel guilty if he continues to want anything that is a day old or older. Here again we feel the prodding of the overarching and undermining political consciousness, preparing us to think we need, and to consent to, a massive mechanization—an unending expansion of the economy even at the threat of monetary inflation and budget deficits. The advance is at all costs, on principle.

With this goes a growing carelessness about being ethical, so ethics, with its constraints on unfair dealing with *individual* persons suffers the same general disintegration marked above. (Whether this is an effect or a cause of the political drive is a question; but that they attend one another is beyond reasonable doubt.) The new saviors of humanity are so willing, even determined, to maul humanity beyond all recognition as a necessary first maneuver towards the final salvation of the remains. If they, the saviors, ever accomplish this mission of salvation, it will take, in the end, a veritable resurrection of the dead People they have slain *en route*, while gradually mortifying themselves unawares. (Please get that etymological sense of "mortify.")

CPSIA information can be obtained
at www.ICGtesting.com
Printed in the USA
BVHW031940300619
552316BV00003B/6/P